# ROYAL CHILDREN

*Above: Edward VI, by Holbein*
*Overleaf: Queen Elizabeth II,*
*Prince Philip and their family in the*
*Gallery, Buckingham Palace*

# ROYAL CHILDREN

## CELIA CLEAR

CROWN PUBLISHERS, INC.
NEW YORK

*For Mary, Davy and Anna*

Copyright © 1984 Celia Clear

First published in Great Britain by
Artus Books Ltd
91 Clapham High Street
London SW4 7TA

Published in the United States of America by
Crown Publishers, Inc.
One Park Avenue
New York, N.Y. 10016

Manufactured in Italy

10 9 8 7 6 5 4 3 2 1

First American edition

**Library of Congress Cataloging in
Publication Data**

Clear, Celia.
  Royal children.

  Includes index.
  1. Great Britain—Princes and princesses—
Biography.  2. Windsor, House of.  I. Title.
DA28.3.C45  1984  941.08′092′2 [B]  84–12165

ISBN 0–517–55361–9

*Below left: Prince Albert (left), later George VI, and his elder brother Prince Edward in 1902.*
*Below right: the daughters of George VI, Princesses Elizabeth and Margaret, in 1935.*
*Opposite: The eldest children of the eldest daughter: Prince Charles holds Princess Anne's hand.*

# CONTENTS

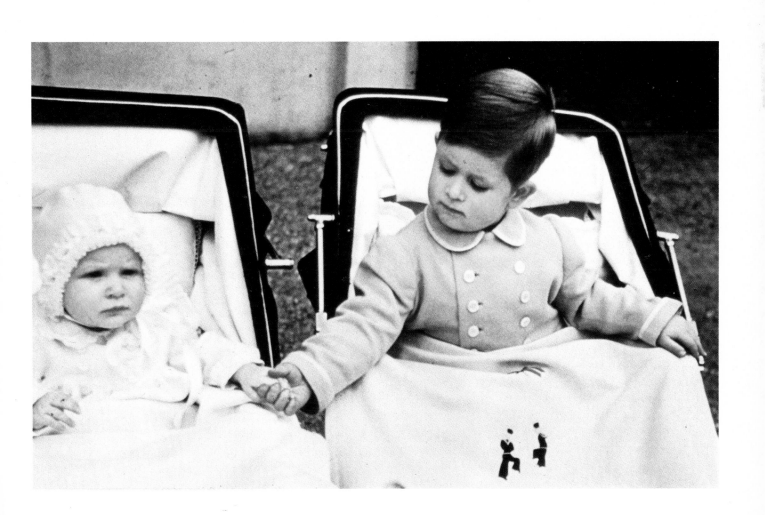

# 1

# BOY KINGS AND CHILD BRIDES

Little Prince William will not be a boy-warrior, nor be imprisoned in the Tower by a wicked uncle, but still he will share many of the problems and pastimes of royal children long ago.

For though centuries have passed since young Edward V was told 'look ye be not caught leaning on the table', the demands made on royal children have scarcely changed. Impeccable manners are terribly important; fluency in languages is very useful; excellent horsemanship, physical stamina, and a sense of style are just as necessary now as they were to princes in medieval times. And although Prince William will grow up in less physical danger than his predecessors, he will have to cope with other strains, such as the ever-curious media, which they never dreamed of. To help him, however, he does have the enormous supporting cast of the whole royal family and the parliamentary system. If a dreadful tragedy were to make him king tomorrow he need not fear that the present Richard of Gloucester would usurp his place, nor that the Kentish men would assemble at Blackheath to march on London. His predecessors may not have experienced jet-lag by the age of one but history had much worse things in store for them.

Life expectancy was so short in the Middle Ages that princes frequently became king at a very tender age. Henry VI was only nine months old when he succeeded Henry V in 1422, and he attended his first Parliament as an infant on his mother's knee. When he was seven he was crowned in Westminster Abbey and presumably after enduring the long ceremony he was given a share of the magnificent sweetmeats prepared for the celebrations,

*The birth of Henry VI at Windsor Castle on 6 December 1421. His father Henry V married a Frenchwoman, Katherine of Valois, after the English victory at Agincourt. A year after his birth their son was King of both France and England.*

including a sugar model of himself with two saints.

Henry's governor, the Earl of Warwick, was empowered to teach him manners, literature and language 'and to chastise us from time to time according to his discretion'. He showed such enthusiasm for the last duty that Henry complained to the Council but alas it only confirmed Warwick's authority. Unfortunately the young King had no mother love to compensate for the strictness of his upbringing because Queen Catherine had retired to Wales to marry Owen Tudor and saw little of her first-born.

Forty-five years earlier Richard II had been rather less unlucky. The son of the Black Prince and grandson of Edward III, he had enjoyed nine years of happy childhood before the deaths of his father and grandfather brought him to the throne in 1377. His mother, gentle Joan of Kent, was highly

*Princess Mary, eldest daughter of Charles I, was married at the age of nine to William of Orange, five years her senior. They were painted by Van Dyck at the time of their marriage in April 1641. Mary left England for The Hague and ten years later gave birth to a son, the future William III of England.*

*Above: an illustration from Froissart's* Chronicles *(above) shows the fourteen-year-old*

*Richard II meeting Wat Tyler at the climax of the Peasants' Revolt in 1381.*

respected and the will of the Black Prince left Richard in her care. He was fortunate too in the loyalty of his uncle John of Gaunt and his tutor Simon Burley. But neither of these two men could turn Richard into a reincarnation of his father, who had distinguished himself on the field of Crécy at only fifteen. Richard was intelligent but neither sport nor fighting attracted him and he grew up aware of his tutors' disappointment. It left him with the arrogance born of an inferiority complex, and when he did come to power he sadly misused it.

In his youth, however, Richard did have one moment of true glory. In 1381 thousands of rebellious peasants marched on London demanding that the King should redress their grievances. Since the Army was in the north fighting the Scots, the King's advisers

*Edward V, when Prince of Wales, is shown standing to the right of his father, King Edward IV. His mother, Elizabeth Woodville, stands behind while her brother, Earl Rivers, presents a copy of Caxton's* Dictes and Sayings of the Philosophers *to the King.*

*Opposite, below: Isabelle of France, only seven years old, is greeted by her betrothed husband Richard II, then already her senior by over twenty years.*

could think of no way to save the city from destruction other than to send the fourteen-year-old monarch to Mile End to negotiate with them. At the first meeting he promised to grant their every demand and many peasants returned homewards, but a dissatisfied core gathered the next day at Smithfield and the King rode out to talk with their leader, Wat Tyler. 'Brother, be of good comfort and joyful', said Wat, 'for you shall have in the fortnight that is to come, praise from the commons even more than you have yet had, and we shall be good companions'. Richard's attendants were so enraged by Wat's condescending speech and further demands that a fight soon broke out. Mortally wounded, Wat rode back towards the massed peasants, crying out for blood. But before their arrows could fly through the air Richard rode towards them shouting 'Sirs will you kill your King? I am your King, I your captain and your leader. Follow me into the fields.' Moved by this appeal the mob quietened and followed Richard out

into Clerkenwell Fields, where the London militia herded them into pens and the revolt came to an end. Although only the ringleaders were treated harshly, none of Richard's promises was kept and while, at only fourteen, he cannot be held responsible for this, he did unfortunately learn that deceit and betrayal sometimes pay off – in the short term.

Richard's second wife, Isabelle of France, was the youngest of seventeen foreign princesses brought to England before 1500 to become queen consorts. Usually they were aged between ten and fifteen, but poor Isabelle was only seven when she crossed the Channel to meet the royal stranger to whom she was betrothed. At her father's court, however, she had shown no fear of the coming match. She told Richard's ambassadors (but was this training or true pride?) 'An it please God and my lord my father that I shall be Queen of England, I shall be glad thereof for it is showed me I shall then be a great lady.'

Isabelle became genuinely attached to Richard, then in his thirties, and despite the rebellious state of the kingdom he made time to visit her at her different castles bearing welcome presents for a young girl. When he departed for Ireland to raise support she wept as if it were their last meeting – as alas it proved to be. At twelve Isabelle was a widow and returned to France.

One English princess, Joan, daughter of Edward III, was only four when she was taken to Germany to be groomed for marriage to the Duke of Austria. A year later, however, the alliance was broken and Joan was sent back home. At the age of fourteen she set out again, this time to marry Prince Pedro of Spain, but was struck down by the plague before the marriage had taken place. 'Whilst me, with parental affection, thought to have had an adopted son to our mutual comfort', wrote Edward III sadly when he heard of the death, 'behold! – with what sobbing sighs and a heavy heart, we sorrowfully relate – death, terrible to all the kings of the earth ... has removed from your hoped-for embraces and ours, our aforesaid daughter; in whom all gifts of nature met.'

Princess Joan's story is a very sad one, but this was not as heartless a way to treat a princess as it appears at first sight. Since these girls were doomed to spend their lives in foreign countries it was much kinder to have them raised in the customs and language of their future homes than to exile them at a later age. When, five hundred years on, Queen Victoria married her seventeen-year-old eldest daughter to the German heir, it was already too late. Poor Princess Vicky was homesick all her life.

The saddest royal children in all English history must be the uncrowned Edward V and his brother Richard, known as 'the Princes in the Tower'. They were twelve and ten when their father Edward IV died suddenly in May 1483. The heir to the throne had been living with his own small court at Ludlow Castle on the Welsh marches, and his father's rather vague instructions for his education record that after Matins, Mass and breakfast he was to receive 'such virtuous learning

as his age shall now suffice to receive'. During lunch he was to listen to 'such noble stories as behoveth a prince to understand'. Then came more study, and exercise before Evensong and supper. Only then was he allowed 'such honest disports as may be conveniently devised for his recreation'. Prince Edward had apparently flourished under this regime for an Italian visitor described him in glowing terms: 'In word and deed he gave so many proofs of his liberal education, of polite, nay rather scholarly attainments far beyond his age.'

This precocity may have contributed to the young King's untimely death, for he was no helpless infant who would serve as a useful figurehead to a power-hungry uncle. At twelve he was nearly adult and though his father left him to the protection of his uncle Richard of Gloucester, Richard may have feared the young King would soon be in a position to turn against him. Another misfortune was the hatred most English nobles felt for his mother, Elizabeth Woodville, who, not content with rising from lowly beginnings to a consort's crown, had schemed to bring all her relatives with her.

Nevertheless it was at first assumed that Edward would succeed his father and he set out for London in the care of his maternal uncle, Lord Rivers. At Stony Stratford his party was met by Richard of Gloucester, who arrested Rivers and his companions and took the King under his 'protection'. Uncle and nephew clashed at their first interview when Edward boldly stated that he intended to entrust the government to the peers of the realm and the Queen, only to be told women had no business in government. Perhaps it was this meeting which convinced Gloucester that he must displace his nephew if he was to survive himself.

However, for a while longer he kept up the pretence that he was 'sure and fastly faithful to his prince', and plans went ahead for the coronation on 24 June. But the widowed Queen had no faith in Richard's loyalty and took sanctuary at Westminster with her

*Once imprisoned in the Tower, Edward V and his brother Richard could only await their fate. A painting by Paul Delaroche in 1831 captures their feelings of fear and helplessness.*

second son and her five daughters. Then rumours of a conspiracy between the Queen and the influential Lord Hastings caused Richard to abandon all thoughts of allowing his nephew to be crowned. Hastings was assassinated, the younger Prince forced out of sanctuary, and the whole royal brood declared bastards through an old scandal which invalidated their parents' marriage. By now all those loyal to the young King were imprisoned or dead, and to avoid civil war and the Woodvilles' supremacy, the Lords and Commons offered Richard the throne. On 6 July Richard was crowned in great pomp and glory while two small boys looked hopelessly out through the barred windows of the Tower of London.

'Alas, I would my uncle would let me have my life yet, though I lose my kingdom', Edward is reported as saying in Sir Thomas More's account of the crime. But More was writing forty years later, under the Tudors, with every encouragement to blacken the name of the last Yorkist king. His story, said to have been the confession of Sir James Tyrell, is that Richard asked Tyrell to have the boys secretly murdered. Two men came into their chamber at midnight 'and suddenly lapped them up among the clothes, so bewrapped them and entangled them, keeping down by force the feather bed and pillows hard unto their mouths, that within a while, smothered and stifled, their breath failing, they gave up to God their innocent souls unto the joys of heaven.' The bodies were buried 'at the stair foot, meetly deep in the ground, under a great heap of stones'.

There has been much discussion over the years as to whether Richard really was responsible for the boys' disappearance. If he was, why did Elizabeth Woodville let her daughters join him at court less than a year later? And why did Henry VII not use the brutal murder as a propaganda weapon against his rival? Did he in fact find the Princes alive in 1485 and do away with them himself?

One telling piece of evidence against Richard was the discovery in 1674 of two child skeletons during the demolition of a staircase outside the White Tower. In 1933 a medical examination suggested the skeletons belonged to two boys aged about twelve and ten, tallying with the ages of the Princes in the autumn of 1483. There is also the fact that if they had been alive when damaging rumours began to circulate, Richard would surely have produced them to clear his name. Perhaps most significant of all though is the chilling report of Dominic Mancini, an Italian priest, who left England in July 1483 with this information on the unhappy Edward:

He and his brother were withdrawn into the inner apartments of the Tower proper, and day by day began to be seen more rarely behind the bars and windows, till at length they ceased to appear altogether. A Strasbourg doctor, the last of his attendants whose services the King enjoyed, reported that the young King, like a victim prepared for sacrifice, sought remission of his sins by daily confession and penance, because he believed that death was facing him.

*Edward VI by Guillim Stretes. He was nine years old when he became King in 1547, but lived for only six more.*

Just seventy years separates the deaths of Edward v and Edward vi but so great was the advancement in learning, literacy and royal record-keeping during that time that we know immensely more about the young Tudor than his Yorkist namesake. No baby has ever been more longed for, plotted for or killed for, than Edward vi. To gain a son Henry viii divorced his first wife and executed his second; while his third, Edward's mother Jane Seymour, died soon after his birth. But despite these tragic beginnings his childhood was not an unhappy one. Apart from his fond though awe-inspiring father he had two doting half–sisters to take his mother's place. His birth had dispossessed both Princess Mary, now in her twenties, and Princess Elizabeth, only four years his elder, but neither showed any jealousy. When he was a baby Elizabeth made him fine cambric shirts, but soon she found he was not a pretty toy but her intellectual rival, and though she was a prodigy of learning herself she soon had to struggle to keep ahead. Princess Mary, a loyal Catholic, hated to see him raised in the new Protestant faith, but nonetheless plied him with affection, presents, and good advice. He also became very fond of his last stepmother, Catherine Parr, Henry's sixth wife.

But when Edward was nine years old his father died and, as usual in minorities, the lords plotted over his person and his power. Within three years one uncle was executed, another in prison, and Edward was in the hands of the Earl of Warwick. He exerted some influence, especially in Church matters, but Warwick wielded the real power and early in 1552 Edward was persuaded to sign the death warrant of his second uncle, Somerset, who had been his Lord Protector. Edward was a serious and contemplative boy and perhaps the death of this loyal man weighed on his conscience, for his health, never good, worsened that spring. By the summer of 1553 he was covered with ulcers and struggling for breath. 'Lord God, deliver me out of this miserable and wretched life, and take me among Thy

chosen,' he prayed. 'Defend this realm from papistry and maintain Thy true religion, that I and my people may praise Thy holy name.' In July he died.

Playing on Edward's love for the new Church, Warwick, now Duke of Northumberland, had persuaded him to leave the throne in his will to his cousin, Lady Jane Grey, who was safely married to Northumberland's son. It was as good as signing her death warrant. The true heir was

*James VI of Scotland at the age of eight. He was the most successful of the boy kings, surviving to become James I of England in 1603, on the death of Queen Elizabeth I. This painting is attributed to R. Lockey.*

*The five eldest children of Charles I. Princess Mary (see also page 7) stands to the far left, and to her left are Prince James, Prince Charles (later Charles II), Princess Elizabeth and Princess Anne. Painted by Van Dyck in 1637, the picture hung over the table in the King's Breakfast Chamber at Whitehall.*

Edward's Catholic half-sister Mary, and she quickly established her authority. Within a year Jane Grey was executed, although she had been only a helpless fifteen-year-old in the hands of unscrupulous men.

Mary, Queen of Scots, the cousin of Edward VI, gave birth in 1566 to the most successful of all boy kings. Crowned James VI of Scotland at one year old, he survived not only to govern his own country but to become King of England too, on the death of Elizabeth I in 1603. His childhood, however, was as troubled as those of his predecessors. During the first year of James's life his mother lost the support of most of the Scottish lords, abdicated the throne in his favour and fled to England. He never saw her again, and heard only critical and

spiteful stories of her from the lords in whose power he lay. By the time he was fourteen he had been in the charge of four regents each of whom died an unnatural death of assassination or execution. James was mostly left unharmed to pursue his studies at Stirling Castle but he lived in constant fear of kidnap by one party or the other, as indeed did happen twice. He grew up devoted to learning and to the Church, with a fear and hatred of violence, and a longing for affection.

The first person to show James any real warmth was his cousin Esmé Stuart who arrived from France when James was thirteen. Demonstrative and merry, where James's Scottish companions were dour and sober, Esmé aroused the deepest devotion in the young King and they were

rumoured to have a homosexual relationship. But within two years jealousies were aroused among other noblemen resentful of James's attachment to Esmé and he was forced to send him back to France. In adult life James made a happy marriage with Anne of Denmark and fathered a brood of children, but he never lost his delight in the company of amusing young men.

James VI and I was the last of the boy kings and his granddaughter Mary was to be the last child bride. The fashion for very early marriages was disappearing but the need to gain Protestant allies forced Charles I to marry his much-loved daughter to William of Orange at the age of nine. At least it meant she was safely in Holland when

the Civil War broke out and she escaped the adventures of her brothers and sisters during the exciting and tragic years which followed.

After the Restoration royal children no longer lived in fear of ambitious uncles or child marriages, although there were still many young lives which were cut short by medical ignorance, or marred by parental discord. Where marriages were happy, however, as with George III and Queen Charlotte, close family life began to develop along the lines which we regard as natural nowadays. But it was with Victoria and Albert that the modern age really began and in the traditions they established lie the strength and unity of the royal family today.

*Queen Charlotte with her two eldest sons in fancy dress, painted by Zoffany in 1764. During her long and happy marriage to George III she produced fifteen children including Edward Duke of Kent, the father of Queen Victoria.*

# 2

# SAILOR SUITS AND STRAW HATS

'O Madam it is a Princess,' said the doctor attending Queen Victoria's first birth in 1840. 'Never mind, the next will be a Prince,' she replied firmly. And indeed within a year she had produced a healthy Prince of Wales. Her first child was named after her, but always called Vicky, and the second was named after her adored Albert, and known as Bertie.

The Queen would have been very happy to rest awhile after these first two fruitful years of married life but Princess Alice appeared in 1843 and Prince Alfred a year later. Then at two-year intervals came Helena, Louise and Arthur, followed by Leopold in 1853 and Beatrice in 1857. It was a large family even by Victorian standards and although there were some satirical cartoons in the radical press, popular ballads applauded the royal fertility:

Here's to the Queen and Albert gay
And all the children too, hurray
May another come the first of May
For another royal christening.

Queen Victoria had been an only child and her father had died when she was a baby, while Prince Albert had grown up with one brother in a broken home, but together they proved to have a genius for family life. Discipline was strict by today's standards but the children's lives were enriched with music-making, amateur theatricals, riding expeditions, sailing trips, swimming lessons, gardening, and a host of other activities, all shared with their ever-loving, ever-anxious parents. The Queen's guiding principle was: 'That they should be brought up as simply as possible and that they should be as often as possible with their parents (without interfering in their lessons) and place their greatest confidence in them in all things.'

*Victoria liked to watch her first baby being bathed and made this sketch of the bedtime ritual (left). 'Pussy' was her nickname for Vicky as a little girl.*

*The Queen's eldest son, Albert Edward, Prince of Wales. When a sailor suit was specially made for him to wear on the royal yacht it set a fashion for children which lasted fifty years. Winterhalter painted him in it.*

*Prince Albert thought it very important that Victoria's subjects should have lots of opportunities to see the growing family, and this was the first of several railway carriages which carried the children from one end of the kingdom to the other.*

Although the writing is Victoria's, the idea was Albert's, as were most of the ideas on the upbringing of the children. In later years the Queen told her eldest daughter that before meeting her husband she 'did not know what a happy domestic life was! Consequently I owe everything to dearest Papa. He was my father, my protector, my guide and adviser in all and everything, my mother (I might almost say) as well as my husband.'

Unfortunately not even Prince Albert could persuade Victoria to enjoy child-bearing, though he gave her the tenderest care during pregnancy and was at her side throughout each birth. 'I don't know what I should have done but for the great comfort and support my beloved Albert was to me during the whole time', she wrote after the birth of her eldest son. As soon as chloroform was introduced Albert encouraged Victoria to try it and the births of Leopold and Beatrice were greatly eased by its comforting effect.

Unlike most mothers, Victoria did not forget her sufferings in rapt adoration of the newborn. 'An ugly baby is a very nasty object', she recorded, '– and the prettiest is frightful when undressed – till about four months; in short as long as they have their big body and little limbs and that terrible frog-like action.' She never dreamed of breast-feeding her children, that would have been far too animal-like for her feelings of propriety. Fortunately Prince Albert loved his babies and was the most frequent visitor to the nursery. He once built a house of bricks so tall that he had to stand on a chair to finish it, and he would play the organ with a baby bouncing on each knee. He believed in vaccination, a sensible diet, and sunny, airy rooms for the nurseries. In matters of discipline he would beat the boys under severe provocation but the girls were usually confined to their rooms.

Vicky, the Princess Royal, spent hours of her childhood isolated in her room contemplating her misdeeds. Although she was merry, bright and affectionate she had the most wilful nature and was given to tantrums when her wishes were crossed. She once apologised for misbehaviour to

*The happy domestic life of Victoria and Albert was a popular subject for prints and sketches. The emphasis they placed on a normal family environment paved the way for the relaxed childhoods of modern royal children.*

THE QUEEN AND PRINCE ALBERT AT HOME.

*Vicky, the Princess Royal, painted by Ross in Turkish costume, a style well suited to her imperious and wilful nature.*

the Princess Royal, though ten years younger than him, guided him round the Crystal Palace with perfect confidence and dignity.

Alas the Prince of Wales, though equally given to tantrums, ·was not equally endowed with brains. Historians have often criticised his parents for burdening his childhood with too much study and too much discipline, but what were they to do with an heir to the throne who was not only backward but idle, rude, violent and dull? It is possible that too much was made of Vicky's cleverness early on, so

her governess Lady Lyttelton by saying 'I am very sorry, Laddle, but I mean to be just as naughty again.' However, she was so engaging in a good mood that no one could remain angry with her for long. Indeed her parents took an immense pride in her cleverness – by the age of seven she could converse easily in three languages and she proved to have a natural feel for politics which delighted her father. Before she was ten years old Albert already nursed hopes that she might one day marry the heir to the Prussian throne and so take his liberal ideas into the heart of reactionary Germany. The lucky man, Prince Frederick William, was invited over to see the Great Exhibition in 1851 and

that even before he began lessons he had already developed an inferiority complex. Certainly by the age of five he was exasperating the devoted Lady Lyttelton with his 'wilful inattention and constant interruptions, getting under the table, upsetting the books and other *anti-studious* practices.'

Two years later his first male tutor found him 'extremely disobedient, impertinent to his masters and unwilling to submit to discipline'. When he was ten a tougher man was appointed, but proved no more successful. A despairing entry in his diary reads: 'A very

bad day. The P. of W. has been like a person half silly. I could not gain his attention. He was very rude, particularly in the afternoon, throwing stones in my face.'

Victoria and Albert were dreadfully disappointed. She had wanted to see her husband reproduced in her son and instead he seemed to have inherited all the weaknesses of her dissipated Hanoverian uncles. Prince Albert had dreamed of raising the perfect modern king, wise, calm, profound, with energy, vision and an impeccable moral character. Unfortunately

*The children were trained from an early age always to be at their ease on formal occasions. The opening of the Great Exhibition on 1 May 1851 was such an event, and one Vicky and Bertie always remembered. The public loved to see the Princes and Princesses behaving with an assurance beyond their years, but, as on this occasion, it was the two eldest who performed most of the public duties.*

*The family at Osborne, May 1857, photographed by Caldesi. From left to right: Alfred, Prince Albert, Helena, Arthur, Alice, Queen Victoria with Beatrice, Victoria, the Princess Royal, Louise, Leopold, Albert Edward, Prince of Wales.*

Bertie was both bad and boring. His only interest was in clothes and his only good points were an affectionate nature and easy social manner – when he chose. No wonder his mother's diary nearly always refers to him as 'poor Bertie'.

She had much greater pleasure from her other three sons, Alfred, Arthur and Leopold. Alfred, 'dearest Affie', was much more lively and clever than the Prince of Wales and pleased his mother when he was fourteen years old by writing a little musical piece for her birthday which he played to her on his violin. Only a few months later she was heartbroken by Albert's decision that Alfred should join his first ship. He had always wanted to join the Navy but the life of a midshipman must have seemed very tough after the comforts of home. 'Dearest Affie is gone', wrote the Queen, 'and it will be

ten months probably before we shall see his dear face which sheds sunshine over the whole house, from his amiable, happy, merry temper, and again he was much upset at leaving and sobbed bitterly.'

Prince Arthur likewise had planned his own career from an early age but he was drawn towards the Army. This was possibly the influence of his godfather the Duke of Wellington, whose birthday he shared and after whom he was named. When Arthur was only two the aged Duke showed him all over Apsley House on the thirty-seventh anniversary of Waterloo. Wellington died soon after but Arthur always retained a great admiration for him and later collected Wellington mementoes and studied his campaigns. In plays and charades Arthur always liked to be a military character and when he was only three he enjoyed

*Bertie, below right, and above with Prince Alfred (pictured left) and one of the long-suffering tutors who did their best to educate him. He was the heir to the throne and yet the most difficult and disappointing of all Victoria's children. The Queen was unimpressed in every way by her eldest son, and described him as having a 'dull, heavy, blasé look'. Below, left: Alfred, nicknamed Affie. He was a much brighter boy than Bertie but his fond mother tended to exaggerate his musical talent.*

dressing up as a Scots Fusilier to have his portrait painted. A gentle, good boy, Arthur was one of his mother's favourites and the only son who never gave her any cause for anxiety.

Leopold, through no fault of his own, was a constant heartache to her. He suffered from haemophilia, the painful bleeding disease which is carried in the female line but affects only males. Victoria was outraged by the diagnosis because it was entirely unexpected; there were no records of bearers in her family or Albert's. But tragically Vicky, Alice and Beatrice all proved to be unwitting carriers and through them the disease was spread into the royal houses of Europe.

The Queen's love and concern for Leopold did not soften the brutal frankness with which she described her children. As a baby she thought him very ugly; by the age of four there was not much improvement. 'He is tall, but holds himself worse than ever and is a very common-looking child, very plain in face, clever but an oddity.' Fortunately he was the only prince to have inherited in full his father's brains and he could while away the long hours in bed with books. But he hated being so often left out of exciting

*Prince Arthur, 'so gentle, so dear, so good' as a Lady-in-Waiting described him. He was interested in all things military and loved dressing up as a soldier; so it was appropriate for Winterhalter to paint him as a Scots Fusilier.*

*Right: Arthur with Leopold, Victoria's haemophiliac son. 'He is very ugly, I think uglier even than he was', she wrote of him fondly.*

activities and when well he was an extremely naughty child. In later life Victoria found him most companionable and came to describe her ugly duckling as the 'dearest of my dear sons'.

As soon as their nursery began to fill up, Albert and Victoria longed for a private family home, more intimate than Windsor and more secluded than Buckingham Palace. But no sooner had they purchased an elegant, spacious Georgian house on the Isle of Wight than they decided it was too small and pulled it down. Albert himself designed the new Osborne House in the style of a large Italian villa. The children loved going there for it had

2,000 acres in which to walk and ride and wonderful views of the sea with ships sailing in and out of Portsmouth. On their private beach Prince Albert had a sort of floating bath constructed in which they could all safely learn to swim. Government ministers strongly disliked crossing to the island in rough weather but for the children it was a wonderful retreat from London and many idyllic summer months were spent there (see pages 28–9).

From Osborne the royal family sometimes made excursions along the south coast in their yachts *Fairy* and *Victoria and Albert*. In 1846 the Prince of Wales appeared on board in a sailor suit, setting a fashion which was to

*The young Princes perform their public duties: here Bertie and Alfred are visiting Brampton Military Hospital, Chatham, and doing their best to cheer up soldiers wounded in the Crimean War.*

last over fifty years. Queen Victoria noted in her diary how 'Bertie put on his sailor's dress, which was beautifully made by the men on board who make for our sailors. When he appeared the officers and sailors who were all assembled on deck to see him, cheered and seemed delighted with him'.

It must have been an unsettling experience for Bertie to have his public appearances treated with acclaim but in the family to be regarded with pity and despair. Before he was seven he had been cheered in Cornwall as its Duke, in Caernarvon as Prince of Wales and in Scotland as the Duke of Rothesay. Although home life was simple and orderly for the royal children the two eldest were far more involved in state and public occasions than future generations were to be. And they loved it. The Princess Royal proudly told her dresser on returning from an engagement in the City in 1848 with her father and brother that she had been 'the only great lady present'. A dignitary had addressed the seven-

year-old Prince as 'the pledge and promise of a long race of kings', but, as his governess recorded, 'poor Princey did not seem to guess at all what he meant'. Still, he enjoyed the cheers of the crowd as he sailed from Greenwich to St Paul's and his smart black velvet coat must have been a pleasant change from the usual sailor suit.

In 1848 a new costume entered the lives of the princes and princesses when their parents first leased Balmoral Castle and became enamoured of all things Scottish, including the kilt. The Castle had a lovely position on the wooded banks of the river Dee with hills rising all around it, and four years later Victoria and Albert took the opportunity to buy it, together with 17,000 acres of land. Soon, like Osborne, it proved too small and had to be rebuilt, and by 1855 a large romantic castle had risen on the site, all turrets and battlements on the outside and all tartan within (see page 88). Every autumn the royal train would travel northwards, as it still does, bearing the excited children to

*The Queen loved to explore the countryside around Balmoral and would take the children riding, walking and sketching. She is shown here with Vicky and Bertie at Loch Laggan. It was pictures like this that helped to increase the popularity of the kilt.*

## QUEEN VICTORIA'S FAMILY AT OSBORNE HOUSE

The present Osborne House on the Isle of Wight was designed in 1845–8 by Thomas Cubitt, the pioneer of modern building methods, under the direction of the Prince Consort. It was a paradise for the royal children. Apart from the endless opportunities for yachting and sailing, they had within the grounds a miniature fort, a carpentry bench for the boys, and the prefabricated Swiss Cottage imported by Albert from Germany. It had its own kitchen (opposite, above) so that the girls could learn to cook and clean. Below that is the garden shed housing the children's miniature tools and wheelbarrows, all bearing their owner's initials; all the children were given every encouragement

to cultivate their own patches of ground.

After the death of Queen Victoria none of her family wanted to take over the house, despite its lovely Italian garden and view across the Solent. So while some of the house was used as a naval cadet school, and is now a convalescent home, the royal apartments were preserved just as they were at the time of the Queen's death. Her sitting room, right, is an example of the contemporary fashion for crowding in photographs of beloved members of the family.

Left, Queen Victoria in the grounds in 1887 with two of her children, now grown up: Arthur, Duke of Connaught, sits on her right, and Beatrice has her back to the camera. With them are children of Alfred, and of Alice; Beatrice's own son, Prince Alexander, is in the arms of the nurse, right.

*Dressing up for charades and tableaux was a part of family life which all the children loved. Above: Alfred and Arthur in Sikh dress at Osborne in September 1854.*

the wild beauty of the Scottish highlands.

The whole family was kitted out in highland dress, studied a little Gaelic, practised reels and strathspeys, went stalking and fishing, visited local tenants, and explored the beauty of Deeside. Victoria grew increasingly ambitious in her expeditions and liked to have the children with her. In 1859 Helena and Louise travelled thirty-five miles with their parents, riding nineteen of them through the most glorious and wild scenery. 'The little girls were in great glee the whole time', recorded the Queen.

When the children had grown out of the ugly baby stage and not yet become annoying adolescents, Victoria enjoyed their company very much, but her obsession with Albert prevented her getting as close to them as perhaps

she could have done. She quite simply thought that none of them was a patch on him, and didn't hesitate to say so. '*None* of you', she wrote, 'can *ever* be proud enough of being the *child* of such a father who has not his *equal* in this world – so great, so good, so faultless. Try ... to follow in his footsteps and don't be discouraged, for to be *really* in everything like him *none* of you, I am sure, will ever be.' Surprisingly it was the reserved, overworked Prince Albert who found it easier to relax with the children, flying kites, collecting shells, building bonfires, skating on the lake at Windsor. He also took them to the zoo and the pantomime, to circuses and theatres and brought conjurers and actors to Windsor to entertain them.

Of course, in the best Victorian tradition, a lot of family entertainment was home-made. All the royal children were taught the piano and singing, and several, particularly Louise, inherited their parents' artistic gifts. But their most spectacular achievements were when they collaborated in theatrical performances for the royal household. They were taught to perform in French and German, as well as English, and when Bertie was only ten and Vicky eleven they acted scenes from Racine's *Athalie*. Two years later, to celebrate their parents' wedding anniversary, the seven eldest presented a tableau of the Four

*Prince Alfred (left) clad in a tigerskin represents Autumn in the Tableau of Seasons presented by the royal children to their parents at Windsor on 10 February 1854. Bertie and Louise (above) played Winter, and Roger Fenton took the photographs.*

Seasons. Princess Alice came in first representing Spring, scattering flowers and reciting verses; then came Vicky and Arthur as Summer; Alfred wore a panther skin and vine leaves to symbolise Autumn, and Bertie, covered in icicles, acted Winter with Louise. To end, the Seasons gathered on the stage and Helena, clothed in white, pronounced a blessing on her parents.

At the time of this anniversary Prince Leopold was ten months old and there was only one further blessing to arrive in the royal nursery. Princess Beatrice was born in April 1857 when the Queen was nearly thirty-six. 'Mother and baby are doing well', Albert wrote the next day; 'Baby

*Princess Beatrice, the last and much-beloved baby, photographed by Caldesi in her cradle at Osborne in May 1857: she was three weeks old. The cradle had been made for Vicky in 1840 and was used by all Victoria's children and grandchildren.*

*Opposite: Queen Victoria's sketch of her youngest daughter.*

practices her scales like a good prima-donna before a performance, and has a good voice! Victoria counts the hours and minutes like a prisoner. The children want to know what their sister will be called and dispute which names will sound best ...'. In fact, as the youngest of nine, she was inevitably called 'Baby' until she was well into childhood. 'Baby mustn't have that, it's not good for Baby', said the Queen at lunch one day. 'But she likes it my dear', Beatrice replied and calmly helped herself.

Far from being outraged by her precocity, both Albert and Victoria were charmed with Beatrice, 'the most amusing baby we have had', Albert said. She was not in the slightest bit in awe of adults, not even of her stern father. When she was four she told a lady-in-waiting, 'I was very naughty last night, I would not speak to Papa, but it doesn't signify much'.

It was fortunate that Albert found such delight in his youngest daughter for he was about to lose his beloved eldest. All his plans had come to fruition; Frederick William had proposed and been accepted when Vicky was only fourteen, and three years later, in January 1858, the time of reckoning arrived. Everything possible had been done to send her well prepared for her future position; her German was already impeccable, as was the whole family's, and her father had given her special lessons in politics. But still, she was only seventeen and on her last day at home the Queen was overcome with remorse about the marriage: 'After all, it is like taking a poor lamb to be sacrificed', she sobbed. For Albert the wrench was even greater. After seeing Vicky off at Gravesend he went straight home and wrote a touching letter: 'I am not of a demonstrative nature and therefore you can hardly know how dear you have always been to me.'

Bertie too left home in 1858 but only as far as Richmond Park where he was incarcerated in White Lodge with his tutor and three hand-picked young men to be turned into 'the first gentleman of the country'. Since Bertie loved

to be surrounded by society and entertainment he did not respond well to this enforced retreat. A year later Victoria was in despair about him: 'I tremble at the thought of only three years and a half before us – when he will be of age and we can't hold him except by moral power! I try to shut my eyes to that terrible moment!'

She wrote these words in a letter to Vicky but she could be equally damning to Bertie's face, and in February 1860 his favourite sister, Princess Alice, had to soothe him down: 'You must remember she is your mother and is privileged to say such things; and though, as Vicky and I have often and long known, that they are not said in the pleasantest way and often exaggerated, yet out of filial duty they must be borne and taken in the right way.'

Princess Alice came into her own when Vicky left home. She was not quite as clever as her sister, but had a sweeter nature and a quiet charm of her own. Although they were now feeling rather guilty over Vicky's early marriage and anxious to keep Alice to themselves a little longer, Victoria and Albert were already on the lookout for a suitable husband. In 1860 Prince Louis of Hesse was invited to Ascot and Alice was as obliging as her sister in falling in love with the chosen one. In November he returned, proposed marriage and was gladly accepted. 'Such a moment is one most touching and moving to witness for Parents' hearts', wrote the Queen, 'when two such fine and good young beings pour out the first confession of their mutual love'.

A few weeks after the engagement came the last of twenty traditional family Christmasses at Windsor, with the decorated fir trees which Prince Albert had introduced in 1841, the tables piled high with presents, fifty

*Winterhalter's painting of the Princess Royal with her younger sisters Alice, Helena and Louise. Alice was very attached to her elder brother Bertie, and carried his hair in a locket; she was a frequent and calming arbiter in the storms between Bertie and his parents. After Vicky's marriage and departure to Germany the younger girls came in for rather more attention than before, although Helena and Louise inevitably suffered from being in the middle of a large family.*

*January 1858: the wedding of the seventeen-year-old Vicky to Frederick William of Prussia. Afterwards Queen Victoria made this watercolour from memory. The three-tier dress was made of white moire antique and the veil was of Honiton lace wreathed with myrtle and orange blossom. The Queen missed her eldest daughter keenly, and kept up a long and intimate correspondence with her.*

turkeys, a baron of beef and a woodcock pie containing a hundred birds. Albert was at his most relaxed on such occasions, swinging little Beatrice in a table napkin, pulling her across the ice on a sleigh and skating with the elder children.

A year later he was dead, and a pall of gloom had settled over Windsor and all the royal homes. The Prince was only forty-two but he had been overworking for years and during 1861 his health began to deteriorate. Among many other troubles that year was the shocking news in November that Bertie, now in the Army, had enjoyed a

brief affair with an actress. When Albert developed typhoid a few days later he became very depressed and showed no will to survive at all. Princess Beatrice recited French verses to cheer him up and Alice played hymns to give him fortitude but gradually, unresistingly, he slipped away from them. On 14 December 1861 Louise, Arthur and Leopold were brought in to say goodbye to him. Bertie, Alice and Helena stayed with him to the end, unable to believe the head and the heart of the family was leaving them.

Gradually, over ten years or so, Victoria grew into his place and well

deserved her title of 'Grandmother of Europe', but initially her thoughts were only for herself, and the children still left at home were sacrificed to her all-pervading melancholy. Four-year-old Beatrice suffered the most because all the Queen's frustrated affection was directed at her. She wrote to Vicky: 'Sweet little Beatrice comes to lie in my bed every morning which is a comfort. I long so to cling to and clasp a loving being.' Frequently at family gatherings the Queen retreated to 'lunch alone with Beatrice', and the poor little girl was cut off from the more cheerful company elsewhere. Though she was taught to dance there were no more children's balls for her to go to and when she learned to ride her most frequent companion was her mother. Growing up in the shadow of her mother's sorrow Beatrice soon turned from a merry impudent child into a shy, repressed young girl. Recalling her own 'joyous childhood' Princess Alice wrote to her mother, 'I do feel so much for dear Beatrice and the other younger ones who had so much less of it than we had.'

But the Queen made no effort to cheer up the lives of her remaining children, in fact quite the reverse. Tutors were instructed to talk often of 'adored Papa and broken-hearted Mama', and six months after Albert's death she warned the Prince of Wales' tutor that his charge, returning from a trip abroad, must avoid any 'gossiping kind of conversation' and be prepared for 'the cureless melancholy of his poor home'. The only outings for the children in these dark days were sad little ceremonies raising a stone or unveiling a statue to the dear departed. The Balmoral holiday that year was particularly depressing. Victoria rode with the children to the summit of Craig Lowrigan to build a memorial cairn. 'Sweet Baby we found at the top. The view was so fine, the day so bright and the heather so beautifully pink – but no pleasure, no joy! All dead!'

At least Victoria held devotedly to Albert's plans for the children and made no effort to detain Alice at home. In July 1862 she married Louis of Hesse and returned with him to Darmstadt. An early marriage had been Albert's only hope of saving the Prince of Wales from moral decline, and by March 1863 Victoria had found the perfect bride in Princess Alexandra of Denmark. Alfred continued with his naval career and spent most of his time at sea. Arthur, too, escaped the worst of his mother's seclusion for at thirteen he was given his own small establishment at Greenwich under the care of a governor. His early devotion to the Army never faltered and by the age of seventeen he had joined the Royal Military Academy.

Left at home with Beatrice were Helena, Louise, and Leopold. Being simply two more girls in the middle of a large family, Helena and Louise had been rather in the background while

Opposite: the bereaved family photographed around the bust of the dear departed Albert, 'that perfection of human beings' as Victoria once described him. All the children mourned the loss of their beloved father deeply, and Victoria sank into a 'cureless melancholy' that was to cast a blight on the home life of her younger children. From left to right: Alice, Helena, Beatrice, Vicky and Louise.

Little Beatrice became the sole provider of comfort to the grief-stricken Victoria, and the elder woman clung to her daughter both literally and emotionally.

Albert was alive. Louise was very artistic but not as bookish as her sisters and exclaimed on hearing of her father's death: 'O why did not God take me. I am so stupid and useless.' She was very pretty, however, and Victoria took a pride in the admiration she aroused. Helena, though much more devoted to her mother, was described in 1864 with the Queen's usual candour: 'Poor dear Lenchen, though most useful and active and clever and amiable, does not improve in looks and has great difficulties with her figure and her want of calm, quiet, graceful manners.' The sisters were some company for Leopold, kept always at home because of his illness, but he missed his father's intellectual companionship and Arthur's cheerful company. 'He suffers so often, and leads so sad and solitary a life', wrote the Queen to Vicky – but she didn't bestir herself to find ways of cheering it up.

The brightest influence on the lives of the remaining royal children was the warm and radiant personality of their sister-in-law Princess Alexandra. From the first meeting, when she swept the shy Leopold into her arms, she was beloved by them all. And soon there was a new generation of little boys in sailor suits for Beatrice to play with. By the time she was fifteen she had twenty-one nieces and nephews, of whom the least lovable was Vicky's William, the future Kaiser of Germany.

Although Queen Victoria was deeply fond of Alexandra she didn't approve of the whirlwind of society in which the eighteen-year-old Princess spent the the early years of her marriage. With such a lifestyle she felt 'hopes there cannot be', but then depressed herself with the thought that if Bertie and Alexandra had children they were sure to be stupid. 'Are you aware', she wrote to Vicky, 'that Alex has the smallest head ever seen? I dread that – with his small empty brain – very much for future children.'

Unfortunately her fears were not altogether unfounded and Alex-

*The wedding of Bertie, Prince of Wales, to Princess Alexandra of Denmark in March 1863. To the right stand Beatrice with her long hair, and her nephew William, the future Kaiser, who misbehaved throughout the ceremony. At the top right of the picture is Victoria, still in deep mourning for Albert.*

andra's firstborn, Albert Victor, proved more dim and lethargic than his father had ever been. He arrived two months prematurely – after his mother had been enjoying skimming across the frozen lake at Windsor in her sledge chair. The event was so unexpected that the local doctor had to attend the delivery and the lady-in-waiting dashed out to a local draper to buy eight yards of flannel. The child weighed scarcely 3¾lb but he soon prospered. Nonetheless at the christening the Queen found plenty to criticise: 'The poor baby roared all through the ceremony, which none of you did', she wrote to Vicky. 'Alex looked very ill, thin and unhappy, she is sadly gone off.' The Queen's present to her grandson was, not surprisingly, a silver statuette of Prince Albert engraved with a moral verse.

Queen Victoria loved to be present at the births of her grandchildren but by some clever juggling with dates Bertie and Alexandra always managed to avoid this. When a second son was born in June 1865 he was said to be a month premature but the Queen was suspicious: 'It seems that *it is not to be* that I am to be present at the birth of your children, which I am very sorry for.' Queen Victoria had already decided on the names of her future heir without consulting his parents so this time they were swift to announce their own choice, George Frederick, before she could voice an opinion. The Queen was not pleased, though she thought Frederick the least awful and hoped they would call him by that name. 'Of course you will add *Albert* at the end, like your brothers, as you know we settled *long ago* that *all* dearest Papa's *male* descendants should bear *that* name, to mark *our line*, just as I wish all the girls to have Victoria after theirs.' The parents dutifully added Albert (a tradition continued until the birth of Prince Charles) but the boy was 'Georgie' to his family and Albert Victor was always called 'Eddy'.

After two sons came three daughters, Louise, Victoria and Maud. Louise was born in February 1867, while the Princess was very ill with rheuma-tic fever, and it was three months before she could give the baby her usual motherly care. Unlike Queen Victoria, the Princess of Wales simply adored babies, and would always bathe them and put them to bed herself if it were possible. However, she was still at this period enjoying a dazzling social round and although her fever left her with a permanently stiff leg, she learned to dance, ride and skate again as well as ever.

When her last child, John, died within twenty-four hours of his birth, in 1871, she was quite desolate, and blamed herself for bringing on another premature birth by too much activity.

*Bertie and Alexandra with their first-born, Albert Victor, fondly known as Eddy.*

His father was heartbroken too and placed the little body in its coffin himself, and arranged the pall of white satin. Alexandra watched from a window as he walked hand in hand with his two sons in the funeral procession. Eleven years later she wrote to George: 'It is sad to think that nothing remains on earth to remind us of him but his little grave.'

Although the Princess was only twenty-six there were no more pregnancies. This may have been for health reasons, but it may also have resulted from a parting of the ways with her husband. Before her rheumatic fever they had been close and she had kept up with his ceaseless round of amusements. But while she lay in bed seriously ill, Bertie had carried on with his usual entertainments in the most heartless way, and she felt his neglect bitterly. Alexandra was also conscious of the social handicap of her increasing deafness, which was a legacy of the fever. Nor could she conceal from herself that Bertie's infidelities were common knowledge. Altogether, after eight years of marriage, she was completely disillusioned and though she never let it sour their family life, and indeed retained a great affection for Bertie, it was upon her children and her country home of Sandringham that she turned the full force of her affection.

This very ordinary large mansion in Norfolk had little to recommend it except good shooting, but generations of the royal family have become very attached to Sandringham. Perhaps it was its complete lack of grandeur, or taste or historical associations which made it agreeable to a family accustomed to castles and palaces. To the Wales family it became what Osborne had been to Victoria's children, and they spent even more time there because their mother's presence was not so often required in London.

With an adoring mother and an easy-going and often absent father, the five Wales children had a much more relaxed childhood than their father had ever known. 'If children are too strictly or perhaps severely treated',

he wrote to his mother, 'they only fear those whom they ought to love.' So although there was plenty of love around at Sandringham there was little discipline and the Queen was not the only relation to feel some anxiety: 'Such ill-bred, ill-trained children I can't fancy them at all'. Alexandra looked on indulgently as her children rode a pony into the bedrooms or jangled all the service bells at once. 'They are dreadfully wild', she admitted, 'but I was just as bad.'

The two Princes were saved from utter spoiling by their kind but critical tutor the Rev. John Dalton. 'Self approbation enormously strong, becoming almost the only motive power in Prince George', he wrote in his record

*Princess Alexandra plays with the first of her three daughters, Louise, later the Princess Royal.*

book. The problem was that the younger boy was so much cleverer than his older brother that it was only too easy for him to get bumptious. On the other hand, the boys got on well together and when the time came for George to enter the Navy, Dalton was reluctant to see them separated. 'Difficult as the education of Prince Albert Victor is now, it would be doubly or trebly so if Prince George were to leave him. Prince George's lively presence is his mainstay and chief incentive to exertion.' So when George set off for the training ship *Britannia* in 1877, his elder brother went with him and everyone hoped the Navy would have some magical effect on this listless heir to the throne.

Unfortunately there was no one of Dalton's calibre looking after the interests of Louise, Victoria and

*The five children of the Prince and Princess of Wales may look solemn in this photograph but visitors found them as 'wild as hawks'.*

*Prince George, the future King George V, aged two. He and his elder brother Eddy were placed under the tutorship of the Reverend John Neale Dalton, the curate of Sandringham, under whose teaching George's intellectual superiority over his brother became all too evident.*

*The children of the Prince of Wales playing with regular and favourite playmates, the Duke of Teck's family at Chiswick. Prince George pulls along his elder brother Eddy. The girl standing to his right is his future bride, Princess Mary. They were sketched by Ella Taylor in 1872, when Prince George was seven years old.*

Maud. Their mother herself had no intellectual interests and was unconcerned when the governess told her that the Princesses showed no enthusiasm for their books. Nor were they given much social training, apart from dancing and music. Alexandra liked to keep them as a close little trio, always dressed alike, in an unchanging nursery world. In their late teens they were still playing children's games at their parties and referred to themselves as 'Toots, Gawks and Snipey'. Their father loved them in a casual way but he was disappointed that none of them had inherited their mother's beauty.

'Darling Motherdear' was the most important person in the lives of all the children. They would say their prayers with her in the evening, and she passed on to them her own reverence for the Bible. When they were young Princess Alexandra read aloud to them and later on Prince George would read to

her during the daily ritual of hair brushing. Their grandmother was another strong presence in their lives, though they did not see a great deal of her. She had insisted from their infancy that she should be consulted about every step of their upbringing and there were many clashes with the Prince of Wales when he failed to do this. She did however admit that whatever the faults of discipline Alexandra brought up her children to have 'great simplicity and an absence of all pride'.

It was a great wrench for Princess Alexandra to lose her sons to the rigours of Navy life. 'I hate to go past your dear little rooms', she wrote to them, 'where I have so often tucked up my dear boys for the night. Have you got to like your hammocks now and do you sleep well?' She asked Dalton, who accompanied them, to make sure they didn't get grand now they were by themselves, but, as George recalled,

*Prince Eddy and Prince George as naval cadets in 1877.*

*Princess Alexandra, 'Darling Motherdear', with her five children. Their devotion to her was genuine and unfaltering, even when she grew old and deaf.*

there was no chance at all of that among two hundred unknown boys.

It was a pretty tough place and, so far from making any allowances for our disadvantages, the other boys made a point of taking it out on us on the grounds that they'd never be able to do it later on. There was a lot of fighting among the cadets and the rule was that if challenged you had to accept. So they used to make me go up and challenge the bigger boys – I was awfully small then – and I'd get a hiding time and again.

Prince George survived, however, and became a capable sailor who later liked to race his own yacht. Prince Eddy on the other hand remained so backward that the Navy suggested he might return to Sandringham. His parents were indignant at such an idea and instead he and Dalton accompanied Prince George aboard HMS *Bacchante* for a seven-month voyage to the West Indies. This was such a satisfactory solution to the problem of educating Eddy that in 1880 they set out again and made a two-year voyage to Cape Town, Australia, Japan, Hong Kong, Singapore, Colombo, Egypt and Greece. Naval discipline and order suited Prince George and developed his upright, conscientious but rather conservative character. Prince Eddy, however, returned to England nearly as backward as when he set out. 'As nice a youth as could be,' wrote a visitor, 'but! his *ignorance*. Lamentable.' What was even more worrying for his parents was Eddy's apathetic laziness and lack of initiative. He was sent into the Army, but like his father before him he discovered only a taste for women and drink. Queen Victoria was always very kind to Eddy but she must have wondered whether the monarchy would ever survive the reign of this dissipated half-wit. Fortunately for posterity, it was never put to the test. Poor Eddy died of pneumonia in January 1891, and it was his capable younger brother, George, who founded the House of Windsor.

## SANDRINGHAM HOUSE

Sandringham, near Kings Lynn in Norfolk, was the private home of Edward VII and Princess Alexandra; it was always their favourite residence. Lady Macclesfield, the Princess's Woman of the Bedchamber, described it as having 'no fine trees, no water, no hills, in fact no attraction of any sort or kind'. Yet it was comfortable, and was enlarged and modernised in 1870.

A picture of Sandringham in its late-Victorian heyday: the Hall (right, below), taken from the *Illustrated London News* of March 10, 1888, commemorating the Silver Wedding of the Prince and Princess of Wales.

During the war years the Princesses Elizabeth and Margaret visited the land girls at harvest time, 1941 (centre).

The present royal family spend part of every year there, and guard its privacy fiercely; the Queen did however let photographers into the grounds in February 1982 to record the 30th anniversary of her succession (far right). Now a new generation will take advantage of the spacious estate, and above Peter Phillips does just that, as he and his father exercise his pony Smokey.

# THE HOUSE OF WINDSOR

Prince George was twenty-five when the death of his elder brother brought him second in line to the throne. It was a double sadness, for besides losing the companionship of a much-loved brother he also had to relinquish his career in the Royal Navy, which had been the bulwark of his life for over ten years.

In July 1893 both losses were softened by his marriage to Princess Mary of Teck, usually called May, who loved and supported him all his days; despite his crusty temper he never failed to appreciate it. 'My love grows stronger for you every day', he wrote

seventeen years later, 'mixed with admiration and I thank God every day that he has given me such a darling, devoted wife as you are,'

Nearly a year after the wedding Queen Victoria was looking forward eagerly to news of the birth of her first great-grandchild: 'Dear May keeps us waiting a little, but it must be very soon'. Prince George passed the last anxious hours reading *Pilgrim's Progress* and was most relieved when a boy was born late in the evening of 23 June 1894. Queen Victoria was particularly delighted, as there had never been three direct heirs as well as the sovereign alive before, and when photographs were taken of the four generations, she sent them all over the world. Within four days she was on the spot, accompanied by the Tsarevitch Nicholas who was visiting England with his fiancée, her granddaughter 'Alicky' of Hesse.

I went over yesterday with Beatrice, Nicky, Alicky &c to see May & the Baby who is a vy fine strong Boy, a pretty Child. May I did not see, as it was rather too soon & the Doctor specially wished she shld be kept vy quiet, but she is perfectly well & Dr Williams said one could not be a stronger & healthier parent than she is – wh. is a gt. thing for the future.

The Queen was very anxious that the baby should be named after her beloved Albert but Prince George and Princess May stuck firmly to their mutual desire to call him after Prince Eddy. He and Princess May had become engaged just before his death and, though there had been no time for a strong attachment to form, she nevertheless revered his memory. So Prince George wrote bravely to his grandmother: 'Long before our dear

*Princess May when still Duchess of York with Edward (known as David), Bertie (the future George VI) and baby Mary.*

child was born, both May and I settled that if it was a boy we should call him Edward after darling *Eddy. This is the dearest wish of our hearts,* dearest Grandmama, for Edward is indeed a *sacred* name to us ....' The Queen could not stand out against this appeal and watched unprotestingly as the future Duke of Windsor was christened Edward Albert Christian George Andrew Patrick David. To his family he was always David.

Queen Victoria was soon presented with a great-grandson Albert, for Princess May's second son was born on the anniversary of the Prince Consort's death and no-one would have dared propose any other name. His parents were afraid the Queen would take against him for invading the doubly sad day, 14 December, on which Princess Alice had also died, but she sensibly wrote that the little Prince was 'rather the more dear to me, especially as he will be called by that dear name which is the byeword for all that is great and good.' However, his maternal grandmother, the Duchess of Teck, wrote prophetically: '*George* will be his *last* name, and we hope some day may *supplant* the less favoured one'. So it proved, for though always known to his family as Bertie, he ascended the throne as George VI.

Bertie was born in York Cottage, an ugly, poky villa beloved of Prince George because it was on the Sandringham estate, not far from the Big

*Edward and Bertie. Prince Edward was always very much the leader, and even when they were adults and faced the Abdication crisis it seemed unthinkable to Prince Albert that he should step into his admired elder brother's shoes.*

House in which he had grown up. As his family increased in size York Cottage proved totally inadequate but though he was occasionally persuaded to look at other property, nothing would shift him. Princess May bore patiently with this absurd situation, as with so many of his prejudices, and in the cramped cottage she gave birth to a girl, Mary, in 1897, and to a third boy Henry in 1900. His godfather the Kaiser welcomed 'a new ray of sunshine in the pretty lodge' but Princess May hoped it was the last sunbeam of her maternal career. Writing to her Aunt Augusta she confessed:

I am just a little bit proud of myself for having another boy which was greatly wished as alas we have so few Princes in our family and now I think I have done my duty and may *stop*, as having babies is highly distasteful to me tho' when once they are there they are very nice! The children are so pleased with the baby who they think flew in at my window and had to have his wings cut off!

*Princess Mary, the only girl among five brothers and, until they went away to naval college, their companion in every escapade. She was her father's favourite child.*

*Above: Prince Albert, later George VI; below, he and his elder brother Edward stand to left and right respectively, with Mary behind and Henry in their nurse's arms, 1900.*

In fact she was to bear two more sons, Prince George in 1902 and Prince John three years later.

Unfortunately Princess May was even less at ease with babies than Queen Victoria had been. Six weeks after the birth of her firstborn she left him with his nurses and had a month's holiday in St Moritz, an extraordinary separation even by the standards of the day. Later she wrote of the baby, 'I really believe he begins to like me at last, he is most civil to me'. Prince George enjoyed taking part in the bath-time ritual but he failed to take the close interest in the nursery that Prince Albert had done, and as a result three years passed before it was discovered that one nurse was actually ill-treating the babies. She was so jealously devoted to Prince Edward that she would pinch him to make him cry before taking him to his parents, and she was so uncaring about little Bertie that her feeding methods left him with chronic gastric trouble. Somewhat late in the day she was dismissed and the younger children enjoyed the kindly attentions of Mrs Charlotte Bill.

The first outside event to ruffle the calm of the royal nursery was news of the Boer War and the early defeats of the British Army. The children's three uncles on their mother's side were all on active service and their letters home were read aloud in the drawing room, while in the nursery Mrs Bill and her assistants pored over sensational newspaper reports. When Mafeking was relieved a great bonfire was lit on the hill above Balmoral just as it had been for the fall of Sebastapol nearly fifty years before.

Queen Victoria lived to see that moment, but not the end of the war. In January 1901 she died at Osborne and the third generation was left to grow up without her guiding hand. She had been very fond of Prince George's children and once recorded in her diary: 'The dear little York children came, looking very well. David is a delightful child, so intelligent, nice and friendly. The baby [Mary] is a sweet pretty little thing.' The three

elder children were taken to the funeral but the Duke of Windsor later recalled that the poignancy of the moment had passed him by. 'I remember now only the piercing cold, the interminable waits and of feeling very lost among scenes of sorrowing grown-up relatives.'

Only a few weeks later there was another major upheaval in their lives with the departure of their parents on an eight-month cruise round the Empire. Until the death of Queen Victoria, Prince George and Princess May had enjoyed the peaceful life of a country squire's family with only occasional expeditions to London, Windsor or Scotland. Now that the Prince of Wales had become King Edward VII they were expected to play a larger part in public life and the Empire tour was the first example of this. Even the detached Princess May found parting from her four children a great wrench. 'Those farewells nearly killed me' she wrote home, 'I am always thinking of the children.' They, meanwhile, were having a splendid time with their affectionate grandparents, Edward and Alexandra. 'I'll look after the young beggars' the King had promised and his ideas of childcare were lots of fun and few lessons. On an outing to Virginia Water David caught a fish and danced for joy: 'This is the first fish I ever caught in my life.' When they went to Sandringham their protesting governess was left behind and they spent a wonderful hot summer playing on the lawns while the adults sat under the trees and watched them indulgently. The happy year ended with the excitement of sailing out on the Royal Yacht *Victoria and Albert* to meet their parents coming home on the *Ophir*, just as Prince Charles and Princess Anne were to do nearly fifty years later. Princess May found that the younger children 'had altered and grown so much that when I got back they seemed like little strangers round the table'. At a family reunion at Sandringham that November, Prince George was created Prince of Wales.

In London Prince George moved his

family into Marlborough House but he refused to take over Osborne on the Isle of Wight and preferred to divide his holidays between Abergeldie Castle near Balmoral and the ever-beloved York Cottage at Sandringham. In these three homes the children

*Prince Henry, Duke of Gloucester. Royal children have always been taught to ride from a very early age.*

*A rare photograph of Prince John (left) and Prince George, later Duke of Kent. George had inherited his mother's brains, and she always found herself most at ease with him and Princess Mary; but he did not follow Prince Henry to Eton, and joined the Navy instead.*

spent most of their time, with occasional visits to Frogmore near Windsor Castle. In many ways it was an idyllic existence. Their tutor Henry Hansell was a kindly, if dull, man who did not overburden them with lessons. Their footman Frederick Finch was part nanny, part friend and kept up with them on long glorious cycle rides around Sandringham. 'The woodland trails of that great estate became for two boys and their sister on rubber tyres an enchanted forest in which almost anything might happen, although it never did,' recalled the Duke of Windsor. At Abergeldie there were picnics at Rob Roy's cave, at Windsor they played hide-and-seek among the marble busts and at Marlborough House there was cricket on the lawn.

Yet a certain anxiety and tension permeated the family life of the Wales children because of the high expectations and frequent rages of their father. He loved them all dearly but he had completely forgotten the fun and frolics of his own childhood and expec-

*Prince Edward in the sailor suit made fashionable by his grandfather fifty years before.*

ted from them the exemplary obedience and smartness of young midshipmen. 'If we appeared before him with our Navy lanyards a fraction of an inch out of place, or with our dirks or sporrans awry, there would be an outburst worthy of the quarterdeck of a warship', recalled the Duke of Windsor. He cared more for their appearance than their educational progress and wrote to David when he was only nine: 'I hope your kilts fit well. Take care and don't spoil them at once as they are new. Wear the Balmoral kilt and grey jacket on weekdays and green kilt and black jacket on Sundays. Do not wear the red kilt till I come'. Even when he was not actually cross with the children he found it hard to unbend. His jokes and teasing were rather heavy-handed and simply made them squirm with embarrassment and become tongue-tied. The

only child who really found the way to his heart was golden-haired Princess Mary, who, though a fearless tomboy, was as pretty and charming a daughter as any father could have wished for.

Princess May did not often come between the children and their father's wrath as she had too great a respect for his authority, but when he was out shooting she enjoyed taking them on pleasant picnics, and while he was working away in the library on his stamp collection she would play whist with them or sing songs around the piano. Emotionally she was too reserved to come close to them but she took a deep interest in their progress and tried to ensure that they did not grow up as ignorant of history and art as their father had done. 'I have taken lately to be present at the boys' history lessons', she wrote to her Aunt Augusta. 'I must say Hansell teaches it

*Queen Alexandra doted on her grandchildren and they found her much more fun to be with than their reserved parents. This painting by Frederick Morgan and Thomas Blinks shows her with Edward, Albert (left) and Mary.*

*The royal children go fishing at Balmoral in 1911. After the coronation of their father they moved from Abergeldie to Balmoral Castle, and in London from Marlborough House to Buckingham Palace.*

well and they really answer the questions very nicely – taking a real interest in what he tells them. This pleases me immensely as you know how devoted I am to history.'

Princess May took a great pride in her eldest son David, who though not a great scholar was handsome, intelligent and charming. Eventually of course she was to appreciate the more lasting qualities of her second son, George VI, but in childhood he was rather a worry to his parents. Sandwiched between an admired elder brother and a petted only sister, he was always overshadowed and a bad stammer discouraged him from speaking up for himself. Perhaps as a result of the frustration this caused, he was disobedient, temperamental and quarrelsome, and very unwilling to concentrate on his lessons. Another handicap was knock knees, a family disability which Prince George was determined should be cured. When Finch once allowed Prince Albert to sleep without the painful correcting splints, he was summoned to the library. Prince George drew his trousers close around his legs and exclaimed: 'Look at me. If that boy grows up to look like this, it will be your fault'. Fortunately Prince Albert's suffering did not prove in vain and eventually the treatment was successful.

The Prince of Wales decided that the Navy would teach David all he needed for kingship and in 1907 he set off for Osborne, which was now a training school for naval cadets. Two years later Prince Albert joined him. The boys' individual tuition at home had not prepared them at all for the competitiveness of school life and their exam results were not encouraging. Prince Edward eventually worked his way up to the middle of the form but his younger brother was invariably near the bottom. His father's letter exhorting him to work harder shows how kindly and concerned he could be, given time for reflection; face to face in the library Prince Albert would have been reduced to jelly but, given

the seriousness of the situation, this letter is really quite tactful:

You know it is Mama's and my great wish that you should go into the Navy and I believe you are anxious to do so, but unless you now put your shoulder to the wheel and really try and do your best to work hard, you will have no chance of passing any of your examinations. It will be a great bore, but if I find that you have not worked well at the end of this term, I shall have to get a master for you to work with all the holidays and you will have no fun at all. Now remember, everything rests with you, and you are quite intelligent and can do very well if you like.

Before Bertie left Osborne to follow his elder brother to Dartmouth the death of Edward VII brought his father to the throne as King George V. In 1911 all the children except the six-year-old Prince John rode in a coach to Westminster Abbey to take part in their parents' coronation. Prince Edward led the peers in making an oath of allegiance to his father, who found it hard not to weep as he kissed the cheeks of his young heir. The next ordeal for the Prince was his investiture at Caernarvon Castle in a

*The four eldest children drill to the sound of pipes. They were under strict instructions from their father on the wear and care of their kilts, in which they were so often to be seen.*

*Queen Mary when still Princess of Wales with her eldest son and Princess Mary. She loved her children dearly but found it difficult to be relaxed and affectionate with them.*

*Princes Albert and Henry and Princess Mary on their best behaviour with their mother at a garden party at Marlborough House in 1907.*

pantomime-style costume of white satin. He enraged the King with his objections to the rig-out and Queen Mary had to exert all her serenity and tact to smooth things over. Finally the Prince of Wales was persuaded to tolerate his costume and despite exhausting heat played his part admirably. The King recorded the event in very moving detail in his diary: 'I put a mantle or robe on his shoulders, a ring on his finger, and a gold rod in his hand, he kneeling before me all the time, then he took the oath of all-

egiance and [I] raised him up kissing him on both cheeks.'

King Edward VII had loved all the pomp and circumstance of monarchy, and King George believed in it, but young Edward's impatience with ritual and dressing up was unfortunately not just youthful rebellion. From this time onwards his refusal to do things in the 'right' way was to cause endless rows and bitterness with his staunchly conservative father. Thanks to the influence of Queen Mary his education was broader than

King George's had been. After making his midshipman voyage he left the Navy and was sent abroad, to improve his languages, and then to Oxford. He had just enjoyed his first London season when the outbreak of war turned his energies towards joining the Army and badgering the authorities to give him a demanding, dangerous job.

Prince Albert was an eighteen-year-old midshipman in 1914 and he had the excitement of serving aboard HMS *Collingwood* at the battle of Jutland. Sadly recurrent stomach troubles disrupted his career and he had to finish his war service in the Royal Air Force. Princess Mary also played her part in the war effort, working as a VAD at Great Ormond Street until 1920. German names became so unpopular during the war that the King changed the name of his House from Saxe-Coburg-Gotha to Windsor.

Mr Hansell had always told King George that the Princes would have made better progress at a preparatory school and the King decided to take this advice for the education of Henry and George. They were both sent to St Peter's Court at Broadstairs but there was no marked improvement in the academic stakes. Queen Mary wrote crossly to Prince Henry: 'Do for goodness sake wake up and work harder and use the brains God has given you .... All you write about is your everlasting football of which I am heartily sick.' And though Prince George became an excellent pianist and inherited his mother's interest in art, he did not shine among the cadets at Dartmouth. 'He has kept up the best traditions of my family', wrote Prince Albert, 'by passing out of Dartmouth one from bottom, the same place as I did.' Prince George nevertheless had to join the Navy, which he never liked, but Prince Henry went from Eton to the Army and took his career very seriously.

The youngest of the flock, Prince John, was a source of great anxiety and sadness to his parents, for at the age of six he developed epilepsy and it retarded his progress. His funny little sayings were much treasured by the family, especially one day when he

*George V's children dressed for his coronation. Standing are Prince Edward, Prince Henry and Prince Albert, while Prince George sits on the floor and Princess Mary on a chair.*

*A year after his father's coronation, Edward was invested as Prince of Wales. He made no secret of his dislike of all the pomp and ceremony, and hated wearing the formal robes, but his mother persuaded him: 'It will be only for this once'.*

watched his mother greet his father and commented: 'She kissed Papa, *ugly* old man.' As he grew older his attacks came more frequently and the other children found it so upsetting that he was sent with the devoted Mrs Bill to live in a farm on the Sandringham estate. In 1919 he died after one of his attacks, aged only thirteen. Queen Mary wrote to a friend: 'I cannot say how grateful we feel to God for having taken him in such a peaceful way, he just slept quietly into his heavenly home, no pain, no struggle, just peace for the poor little troubled spirit which had been a great anxiety to us for many years. . . .' Queen Alexandra had made a special pet of her youngest grandson and in her grief her thoughts went back to the baby she had lost: 'Now our two darling Johnnies lie side by side.'

Four years later the King and Queen welcomed their first grandson, George Lascelles, born a year after the marriage of their only daughter Mary to Viscount Lascelles, later Earl of Harewood. Although the King was very relieved that his daughter had chosen an Englishman rather than a foreign prince, Buckingham Palace seemed very empty without her and the Harewood estates lay far to the north of Sandringham. So he was particularly delighted when in January 1923 his second son, Albert, became engaged to Lady Elizabeth Bowes-Lyon. 'The better I know and the more

I see of your dear little wife', he wrote to Prince Albert after the wedding, 'the more charming I think she is and everyone fell in love with her here.'

Fond though he was of Bertie, now Duke of York, King George had very much feared that he would never win the hand of so lovely a creature as Lady Elizabeth, courted on all sides for her beauty and sweetness of temper. Prince Albert was still painfully shy and had never outgrown his embarrassing stammer. But the quiet determination with which he pursued his suit gradually won first her respect and then her love, and she saw the man he could become in the warmth and security of a happy marriage.

Their first home was White Lodge in Richmond Park but it proved (as Princess Alexandra finds today) irritatingly far from London without offering the privacy of a country home. So while they searched for a house in London they stayed with the Duchess's parents in Bruton Street and here Princess Elizabeth was born by a Caesarian operation on 21 April 1926. Prince Albert wrote to his mother: 'You don't know what a tremendous joy it is to Elizabeth and me to have our little girl. We always wanted a child to make our happiness complete, and now that it has at last happened, it seems so wonderful and strange. I am so proud of Elizabeth at this moment after all she has gone through during the last few days ...'

The Duke and Duchess were given less than nine months to enjoy their baby before the King sent them on a long tour of the Antipodes at the beginning of 1927. For the Duchess it must have been the most dreadful wrench to be parted from the Princess for six long months when she was at such a fascinating age. 'I felt very much leaving on Thursday', she wrote to Queen Mary, 'and the baby was so sweet playing with the buttons on Bertie's uniform that it quite broke me up.' The Duchess's parents, the Earl and Countess of Strathmore, were anxious to look after little Elizabeth but the King was already bewitched by her, so her time was tactfully divided between both sets of grandparents. At Buckingham Palace she entertained the King and Queen every tea time; she was a serene, happy child so unlike their own nervous sons.

King George's eldest grandson George Lascelles found his visits to the Palace most intimidating and came to the conclusion that the King simply did not like children, but this was certainly not true of girl-children. The Archbishop of Canterbury was once admitted to his presence only to find him on hands and knees with the little Princess pulling him along by his beard. And he would make painstaking efforts to sketch pictures for her, only to be told 'you're not a bad drawer'. It was like the relationship between Prince Albert and the baby Beatrice; she was not afraid of him and he was enchanted by it. One Christmas

*Queen Mary with her adored granddaughter Elizabeth in 1927.*

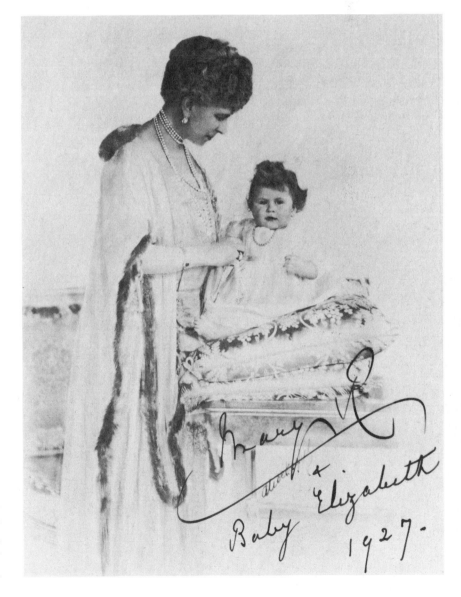

*Princess Elizabeth and Princess Margaret take the air in Hyde Park. Prince Charles was to use the same pram.*

*Margaret Rose selling heather at a garden fete in the grounds of Abergeldie Castle, September 1933. She was the first royal baby to be born in Scotland since Charles I.*

he received perhaps the most treasured compliment of his life when, hearing the carol singers proclaim joy 'to you and all mankind', the Princess exclaimed: 'I know that old man kind. That's you Grandpapa England. You are old, and you are very, very kind.'

Princess Elizabeth's other grandfather, the Earl of Strathmore, owned Glamis Castle in Scotland and here, in the summer of 1930, she and her parents awaited the birth of a new baby. Since the Prince of Wales was still unmarried there was a possibility that the York children might one day inherit the throne and for this reason the royal family would have welcomed a son, to protect Elizabeth from this fate. But the little daughter born on 21 August was so pretty and merry a child that the Duke and Duchess were very content with their small family. They wanted to call the baby Ann but the King had a prejudice against the name and it had to be put on ice until the next generation. By the time they had settled on Margaret Rose it was October and all over the country parents had registered their daughters by surname only until the royal names were announced. It was typical of the enormous interest which surrounded the children at home and abroad. The good-looking parents and charming little girls made an ideal family in which everyone could take pleasure and pride.

*March 1939 (right): the Princesses accompany their parents to Victoria Station, to bid farewell to the French President and members of his suite. By the time they reached their teens the girls were relaxed and assured on such occasions.*

*A rare outing to the zoo (below). The Princesses loved such excursions outside their own familiar world, but public interest made them more and more difficult.*

The Yorks' happiness was no empty façade created for the cameras. In the years between Princess Margaret's birth and the Abdication they led an idyllic existence, partly at 145 Piccadilly and partly at the Royal Lodge in Windsor Great Park. Both the Duke and Duchess placed great importance on a loving, carefree childhood for their daughters: she to recreate the joys of her own youth, he to avoid the miseries of his. 'He was determined', wrote his biographer Sir John Wheeler-Bennett, 'that come what might, Princess Elizabeth and Princess Margaret should look back upon their early years as a golden age.'

They were very concerned to find a governess for their children who would not dull the golden age with boring lessons or too much discipline.

Their choice fell upon Miss Marion Crawford, a young Scotswoman who had been employed by the Duchess's sister. They were impressed not only with her recommendation as a lively teacher but by the fact that she was an energetic walker, well able to keep up with two active young girls. Miss Crawford travelled south with great trepidation expecting to meet 'a couple of very spoiled and difficult people', but liking was mutual and 'Crawfie' was to become a much-valued teacher and friend for sixteen years. Sadly she was persuaded to write her memoirs for an American publisher and the royal family never forgave the breach of confidence. Until that time, however, she proved everything the Duke and Duchess had wished – a sensible, entertaining com-

*Princesses Elizabeth and Margaret take their part in the Silver Jubilee celebrations for their grandfather George V, 1935, in a painting by Frank Salisbury.*

panion who tried hard to keep the Princesses in touch with the real world. Their lessons could have been – should have been, perhaps – more demanding but Crawfie's great contribution was in her encouragement of other activities such as swimming, Girl Guides, amateur theatricals and secret forays into London life.

She knew that a real treat for Princess Elizabeth and Princess Margaret was to ride on top of a bus or drink tea out of thick cups at the YWCA canteen. Queen Mary took her granddaughters on more serious educational outings, to the Tower for example, or to art galleries. 'I was absolutely exhausted', remembered Princess Margaret, 'by hours of walking and standing in museums and galleries. When I grew up I decided my

*George VI towers over his heir and eldest daughter Elizabeth.*

children should never be allowed to see more than three great pictures at a time, so that they would actually plead for "just one more", instead of dropping with fatigue and longing to go home.'

The Duke and Duchess of York spent a lot of time with their daughters. 'No matter how busy the day, how early the start that had to be made', wrote Crawfie, 'each morning began with high jinks in their parents' bedroom.' If the Duke and Duchess were at home they all had lunch together and there were more fun and games between tea and bedtime. On Friday afternoons the whole family drove down to Royal Lodge and spent a relaxing weekend reclaiming its wild garden and riding in Windsor Great Park. Treats were few and far between, but all the more valued for that. After their annual visit to the pantomime Margaret would re-enact every part

for weeks following. A rare public appearance was at the King's Silver Jubilee of 1935 when they drove in the procession to St Paul's, two tiny pink figures waving from an open landau.

The Princesses were usually dressed alike but their characters were completely different. Princess Elizabeth lost some of the spontaneity of her infancy as she grew up and became a reserved, serious child, anxious to meet expectations and to do things properly. Princess Margaret very much minded being four years behind – especially when their nanny 'Alah' tried to baby her in the pram long after she wanted to be running after her sister. She was a mischievous, vivacious child and very devoted to 'Lilibet' although she could not resist teasing her over her excessive tidiness and other virtuous ways. Princess Elizabeth was sometimes shocked by her sister's wilfulness but she took a touching pride in her precocity and never liked her to be left out. Sir James Barrie, visiting them at teatime, noticed the elder sister's pleasure 'whenever the Princess Margaret won a game .... It was like the pride of a mother, though it began, to my eyes, when both were little more than babes.' As they grew older Princess Elizabeth became anxious that Margaret's high spirits should not disgrace her in public: 'If you do see someone with a funny hat, Margaret, you must *not* point at it and laugh', she warned her before a garden party. On the whole, however, they were good companions, complementing each other's personalities and sharing so close an intimacy that perhaps they never minded that they had few other friends. Despite Crawfie's efforts their life was very insular and sometimes Princess Margaret would exclaim 'I want to *know* about people, Crawfie.'

The idyllic years came to an end with the death of their grandfather George v shortly after they had spent a last Christmas together with him at Sandringham. 'Grandpapa has gone to heaven', Margaret remarked philosophically 'and I'm sure God is finding him very useful.' For the nine-year-old

*The Princesses follow their mother out of the royal limousine. They both had a tendency to be carsick and long rides were a great ordeal.*

Princess Elizabeth, however, it meant the loss of a real friend and the solemn funeral service at Windsor was a sad ordeal for her. In the same Chapel her father had watched the funeral of Queen Victoria, thirty-five years before.

The King's death naturally brought Elizabeth nearer to the throne, but she could still have been supplanted by a child of the new King, Edward VIII. The Princess could not have guessed that the elegant American lady he brought to tea at Royal Lodge in the spring of 1936 was to seal the fate of her father and herself. By December Edward VIII had made up his mind to renounce the throne in order to marry Mrs Simpson.

The implications of the move to Buckingham Palace were not lost on the children and they understood that Elizabeth would one day be Queen. 'It's a good thing she's the eldest, isn't

it Mummie', Princess Margaret once said after behaving more outrageously than usual. But that was far away and unreal; the distressing thing was the worried look their father wore, appalled at the responsibility thrust upon him, and the encroachment of state affairs upon the happy family life they had enjoyed. Now the King and Queen were rarely in for lunch, and evening engagements curtailed the bed-time romps.

For the first five months of the new reign the excitement of preparing for the Coronation overshadowed everything else. The Princesses looked entrancing in their robes and coronets and the carriage they shared with Queen Mary inspired even louder cheers than the royal gold coach.

The vastness of Buckingham Palace made the King and Queen particularly aware of the unreality of their children's lives and they wanted them

*The new King and Queen appear on the balcony at Buckingham Palace to receive the cheers of their subjects, after the coronation in 1937. Their daughters were given a particularly warm reception.*

*The Girl Guides had great fun at Windsor, camping in the Great Park and attempting an assault course arranged by the Grenadier Guards. Princess Elizabeth is to the right of the first row and Princess Margaret to the left of the fourth.*

*The Princesses star in* Aladdin *at Windsor Castle, December 1943. Despite the deprivations of wartime, the Castle was not short on silks, brocades, sedan chairs and velvet curtains, all of which made marvellous props and costumes for amateur theatricals.*

to feel more part of the community. One solution seemed to be the formation of a Guide company at the Palace where they could enjoy activities with other children. Miss Violet Synge, invited to be its captain, accepted with much trepidation. How could she recreate the jolly, sisterhood of Guiding behind palace walls? And her worst fears were realised when footmen flung wide the terrace doors and her new recruits came down to meet her: 'fourteen little cousins or friends all dressed in their best, hairs beautifully curled and white gloves completing the bright array.' The only sensibly dressed children were the Princesses themselves, who had assured her they loved getting dirty and wanted to cook sausages on sticks. Gradually she persuaded the other recruits 'to run and climb and to do all the things that the eleven-to-fourteen-year-old is usually all too willing to do', but she never got used to the presence of detectives and sudden appearances of the King and Queen in the midst of a riotous game.

In the spring of 1939 the royal couple left home for a seven-week tour of North America. The two Princesses were touched to receive hundreds of letters and photos with news of their parents, and bundles of cheering comics. They realised for the first time what a warm and personal interest was taken in them by unknown well-wishers far away. When the King and Queen returned they had the excitement of sailing out to meet them on board a destroyer and transferring to the *Empress of Britain* in the middle of the Channel.

A few weeks later they accompanied the King to an inspection at Dartmouth Naval College and Princess Elizabeth met for the first time Prince Philip of Greece, whom she was to marry eight years later. They were distant cousins for he was descended from Queen Victoria's second daughter, Princess Alice, and she of course was the great granddaughter of Alice's elder brother Edward VII. No meeting of true minds was recorded on this occasion but the Princesses, unused to male company, were very impressed with how high Philip could jump and how much food he tucked away. When the royal family sailed off his little dinghy followed them far out to sea, long after most of the flotilla of small boats had turned for home. Princess Elizabeth was thirteen at the time and he was five years older.

Hardly had the King settled into his new job when the outbreak of war cast an additional burden upon him. The Princesses were first sent to Royal Lodge but as the blitz grew worse they were moved to Windsor Castle. Situated only twenty-five miles from London, the Castle was hardly impregnable but the King and Queen wanted their daughters close enough for the family to be together at weekends.

Stripped of its treasures, bristling with anti-aircraft guns and enveloped in the blackout, Windsor was hardly the most cheerful place in which to spend one's teenage years, but Crawfie did her best to cheer up the dark days with new activities. A Guide company was re-formed and enjoyed the whole of Windsor Great Park for tracking, hiking and camping. Evacuee children from London joined it and broadened the Princesses' experience of life considerably. Margaret's patrol was always the most riotous at camp, Crawfie noticed.

Every evening I would watch the same performance. From the tent that housed Margaret there would burst forth storms of giggles. The Guides officer would appear, say a few well-chosen words, and retreat. The ensuing silence would reign for a minute or two, then a fresh outburst probably meant Margaret was giving her companions an imitation of the Guides officer's lecture.

Another bright spot in the lives of the Princesses was acting in the Windsor pantomimes, which were lavishly presented on the stage in the Waterloo Room erected by Queen Victoria for her family's theatricals. Although

*The serious and dutiful eldest daughter among the strawberries and lettuces at Windsor in 1941. It was a grim fortress in which to spend her teenage years.*

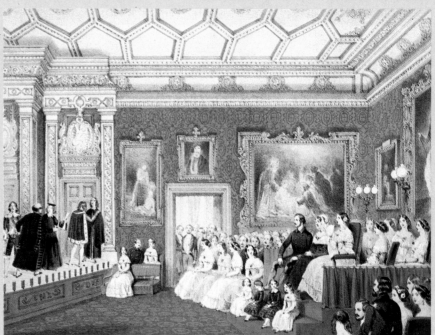

## THE ROYAL FAMILY AT WINDSOR CASTLE

Windsor has been the home of England's Kings and Queens since medieval times. Edward III founded the Order of the Garter there, George III passed his sad, mad last years here, and it was to this Castle that the young Victoria welcomed Prince Albert in 1839.

Victoria's family take the air in 1850 (far left), and near left, centre, watch the first Royal Command Performance in the Rubens room. Bertie, Victoria and Alice sit beside the stage. Helena, Arthur, Leopold and Louise sit in front of their father, grandmother and the Queen.

During Albert's lifetime Windsor became the favourite home for the family Christmas, and it was he who introduced to Britain the German custom of bringing fir trees indoors as the centrepiece for the decorations. Near left, below, is a watercolour of 1850 by John Roberts, capturing the almost magical atmosphere.

Edward VII preferred to spend the annual festivities at his own favourite home, Sandringham, but in recent years it has been Windsor once more. It is the one time of the year when all the members of the family are together: below Lady Helen and Lord Nicholas Windsor and the Earl of St Andrews stand on the steps of St George's Chapel, Windsor.

The present Queen has great affection for the old grey Castle. In July 1941 she was photographed with her sister and mother at their lessons in the grounds (right, above). Her own family now enjoys to the full the many opportunities for sport (right).

*The royal family in 1946. With the war over at last George VI wanted time to enjoy his family in peace and he was reluctant to agree to Elizabeth's engagement to Prince Philip of Greece.*

*Princess Elizabeth in the ATS (Auxiliary Territorial Service) at Camberley in 1945. 'She took immense pride in the fact that she was doing what other girls of her age had to do', Crawfie wrote, 'and apart from coming back to Windsor to sleep, she kept strictly to the routine of the mess, taking her turn with others as duty officer, doing inspections and working really hard on the maintenance of cars.'*

Princess Margaret was always sick with nerves she was a born actress and made a charming Cinderella, with her sister as the Prince. Posters for *Aladdin, Dick Whittington* and *Mother Goose* soon filled the empty picture frames at the Castle and the King took a delight in displaying his 'ancestors' to visitors.

One night towards the end of the war Prince Philip was sitting in the front row. He and Elizabeth had been corresponding in a cousinly way for some time and although preoccupied with his war service he spent the occasional leave at Windsor and grew increasingly attached to the Princess. She had admired him since their first meeting and, despite the series of young Guards Officers stationed at Windsor Castle, her interest had never faltered. In 1944 he asked his cousin King George of Greece to test the water with her father but the reply was not encouraging: 'We both think she is too young for that now. . . . P had better not think any more about it for the present'.

When the war ended the King still wanted to postpone the loss of his daughter. He wanted time to enjoy again 'us four, the Royal Family', without the pressures that had overshadowed his children's growing up. 'Poor darlings', he wrote in his diary on VE night, 'they have never had any fun yet.' But while Princess Margaret, at fifteen, was thrilled with the prospect of the royal trip to South Africa Elizabeth dreaded a four-month separation from Prince Philip. When they returned the King could resist her entreaties no longer and Elizabeth and Philip were married in Westminster Abbey in November 1947. The bride was twenty-one and her little sister a lovely chief bridesmaid at seventeen. The King wrote her a poignant letter of farewell:

Your leaving us has left a great blank in our lives but do remember that your old home is still yours and do come back to it as much and as often as possible. I can see that you are sublimely happy with Philip which is right but don't forget us is the wish of

Your ever loving & devoted
Papa.

# 4

# THE QUEEN'S CHILDREN

The four years between her marriage in 1947 and her accession were very precious to Princess Elizabeth. For this brief span she blossomed as a wife and a mother, unburdened by the cares of kingship. But she was still the King's daughter and in the early months of her first pregnancy she had to go ahead with a hectic four-day official visit to France. Her private secretary Jack Colville was anxious for her health but no trace of tiredness dimmed her sparkle for the French: 'By the time she left Paris, feeling at times extremely ill, the French were absolutely at her feet.'

Within a year of her wedding the heir was safely born on 14 November 1948 in Buckingham Palace. It was not the fashion for fathers to be present and Prince Philip allayed his nerves with a game of squash. Shortly after nine o'clock in the evening the glad tidings were brought to him and he bounded up the stairs with a large bouquet. The cheers and laughter of the crowd outside the Palace carried on so late that eventually police vans had to drive round appealing for quiet so that the newest inhabitant could sleep in peace. There was a special cheer for Queen Mary, then eighty-one, who drove through the gates at 11 pm to see her first great-grandchild. Twenty-four hours later the crowd was still there and singing tuneless lullabies round the Victoria Monument. It had been altogether a noisy day with cannon firing and bells pealing to welcome the future king.

Princess Elizabeth gazed in awe at her baby, not because he was thirty-ninth in descent from Alfred the Great, but with the amazed delight of all new mothers. 'I still can't believe he is really mine', she wrote to a friend, 'but perhaps that happens to new parents. Anyway, this particular boy's parents couldn't be more proud of him.'

When the baby was four days old Crawfie, her former governess, was invited to see him and discovered that, like all the newly-born royal babies she had seen, he bore a strong resemblance to King George V. 'Like the little Kents and the little Gloucesters, this baby also had that absurdly mature look, and ridges under his eyes. He was very healthy and strong, and beautifully made, with a flawless, silky skin.'

The chapel at Buckingham Palace had been bombed during the war so the little Prince was christened in the Music Room, wearing the same robe of Honiton lace which had been worn by all Victoria's children. His names are Charles Philip Arthur George, ignoring Victoria's decree that all her male descendants should bear the name of her beloved Albert. Four of her surviving granddaughters were present and watched the baby christened from the gold lily font which had been made for the Princess Royal 108 years earlier. Princess Elizabeth admired her son's small hands, which were 'fine, with long fingers – quite unlike mine and certainly unlike his father's. It will be interesting to see what they become.'

The birth of Prince Charles aroused enormous interest everywhere. Parcels of beautiful baby clothes were sent from every quarter of the globe, with hand-knitted shawls, coats and bootees. The royal family kept what could be used and made the rest up into layettes for other newcomers. There was a flood of letters enclosing birth certificates from proud parents who wanted to prove that their baby had

*Proud parents show off their baby son, born in the first year of their marriage.*

been born at the same time as the Prince.

Before Prince Charles was a year old his parents were able to move into a home of their own, Clarence House, which had been unoccupied since 1911. A lot of work had been done to make it habitable and especially loving care went into planning the nursery. It was furnished in blue and cream with a pretty chintz of nursery-rhyme figures, and its own small bathroom with child-sized bath and towels. In a glass cabinet stood all the tiny ornaments the Princess had loved as a little girl. Other relics of her childhood were the cot and baby basket, refurbished in yellow silk, and the enormous pram. One of Prince Charles's earliest memories is of lying in its depths with high sides all around him.

Although Prince Philip took great pleasure in his wife and son and Clarence House, he also fretted to resume his naval career and in 1949 he escaped the Admiralty and joined HMS *Chequers*, a destroyer based on Malta. Nowadays it seems extraordinary that Princess Elizabeth didn't immediately set up a nursery in Malta so that the family could be together, but in those days babies were not considered strong enough to withstand changes of climate and the excitement of air travel. So the Princess had to divide her time between husband and son, between Malta and London.

She flew out first in November to celebrate her second wedding anniversary and remained in Malta until the spring. It was a relaxed and carefree time for her, the nearest she ever reached to everyday life. Prince Charles was left in the care of his grandparents, and in his Christmas broadcast George VI made a special

*The Queen plays with her two eldest children at Balmoral.*

reference to his grandson and his mother: 'Here at Sandringham the Queen and I are very glad to have with us both the oldest member and youngest member of our family.' Prince Charles was only four when Queen Mary died but he does remember being taken on visits to Marlborough House and making his bow to the upright figure seated regally in a chair.

When Princess Elizabeth returned from Malta in the spring she was pregnant again, and a daughter was born in Clarence House on 15 August 1950. 'It's the sweetest girl', Prince Philip said on the telephone to his mother but the baby refused from the earliest age to be sweetly feminine. Charles had been a tranquil baby but little Anne was lively and demanding even in her cradle. She was christened Anne Elizabeth Alice Louise. The first name was one which had been vetoed by George v when it was proposed for Princess Margaret; the second was, of course, after her mother and grandmother; the third after her father's mother; the fourth for the Queen of Sweden who was related to both her parents.

The Queen nursed her children in early babyhood, then they were given into the loving care of Mrs Helen Lightbody and Miss Mabel Anderson. Mrs Lightbody came on the sound recommendation of the Duchess of Gloucester but Miss Anderson was completely unused to royal circles. She had advertised for a position in a paper and was amazed to find Clarence House among the replies. The children spent most of their early years in the nursery for their mother could only spare half an hour in the morning and an hour or two in the evening to join them for fun and games. But they also enjoyed a lot of attention from Aunt Margo and their devoted grandparents. At Christmas in 1950, with the Princess once again in Malta, the King wrote to her: 'Charles is too sweet stumping around the room. We shall love having him at Sandringham. He is the fifth generation to live there and I hope he will get to like the place.'

Elizabeth and Philip had shipped

some pictures and furniture out to Malta with the intention of making their villa there a second home in the years to come. But this happy prospect receded as the King's health began to decline rapidly. He had not been well for several years but his family had hoped that with care and attention many years might be left to him. Sadly, however, in the spring of 1951 he was found to have developed lung cancer, and given only two years to live. For the Princess it was a terrible personal shock; for Prince Philip it was also the end of his professional career. With immense regret he relinquished his naval command and returned home to

*Charles and Anne were not always as companionable as this photo suggests. Shy Charles was often outshone by his extrovert, more aggressive sister.*

*The Queen's father and her eldest son photographed together on Charles's third birthday. Greatly treasured by the Queen, this picture still stands on her desk.*

England to help his wife take over more of the royal duties.

In October they flew out to Canada for their first long tour together. They missed Prince Charles's third birthday but the Queen has a treasured photograph of the day showing her son and her father in earnest conversation on a sofa in Buckingham Palace. The family was reunited at Christmas but the King's illness cast a gloom over the usual merriment at Sandringham. In January Charles and Anne had to say goodbye to their parents again, for they were off on the Commonwealth tour which had been planned for the King. He came to the airport to see them off, a brave, frail figure, and then returned to the peace of Sandringham. On 5 February he felt well enough to go out shooting with Lord Fermoy, whose granddaughter Diana (as yet unborn) was to marry his grandson. Back at the house he visited the nursery and heard the children say their prayers. It was the last time they were to see him. The next night their grandmother had to take over the evening ritual for the King had died in his sleep. Prince Charles's sadness that

Grandpapa had gone away was partly offset by the happy news that Mama and Papa were coming back, but he was upset to see everyone in tears and gently urged Queen Elizabeth: 'Don't cry, Granny'.

He was now Duke of Cornwall, Duke of Rothesay, Earl of Carrick and Baron of Renfrew, Lord of the Isles and Great Steward of Scotland. 'That's me, Mummy', he would cry when he heard his name mentioned in Church, though later on, as a schoolboy, it would embarrass him terribly. His parents were in no hurry to make him aware of his destiny. To everyone in the Palace he was simply Charles and Prince Philip would be irritated if he was shown too much deference. 'He's got hands, hasn't he?' he snapped at a footman who leaped to open a door for his son. When asked in an interview many years later to pinpoint the moment he first realised he was no ordinary mortal, Prince Charles said there was no sudden awakening. 'I think it's something that dawns on you with the most ghastly inexorable sense. I didn't suddenly wake up in my pram one day and say "Yippee".'

Nevertheless as preparations began for the Queen's coronation on 2 June 1953 it must have become obvious to the young Prince that his mother was the centre of an unusual and exciting event. She thought he was too young to take the solemn oath of allegiance that tradition demanded and indeed she decided against taking him to the Abbey at all, but the Prince so begged to see her crowned that she relented. His hair was slicked down with a fragrant cream ('Doesn't it smell nice, Granny', he said) and he was dressed in a white satin suit and taken to the Abbey through the back streets. He arrived just as his mother was about to be anointed with oil, and in the midst of this solemn moment the Queen found time to give her son a reassuring smile. The Prince watched eagerly, full of questions for his grandmother beside him, and he was allowed to stay until the actual crowning was over.

*Charles plays with his grandmother and younger sister in the Welsh House, which had been a present to his mother from the people of Wales on her sixth birthday.*

*Prince Charles between his grandmother and aunt Margaret at his mother's coronation. Anne joined the family on the Palace balcony afterwards (below).*

Back at the Palace he and his sister joined their parents on the balcony and looked down for the first time on the sea of madly cheering faces below.

Prince Charles has retained only the vaguest memory of that great day but Princess Anne remembers clearly that she was 'full of sisterly fury at being left behind'. She always minded being the younger one and strove in everything to equal her elder brother. In later life Charles was to become the more sociable of the two but in childhood he was sweet and shy and obedient, while she was noisy, wilful and obstinate. From an early age he displayed unusual thoughtfulness about other people and had impeccable manners. Princess Anne on the other hand could not even be persuaded to curtsey to Queen Mary if she didn't feel like it. When she discovered that the Palace sentries had to present arms each time

she passed them she would go backwards and forwards for the pleasure of seeing them do it. Prince Charles would have been dreadfully embarrassed to put them to such trouble. The Queen and the Queen Mother adored him: in his shyness and sensitivity he reminded them of the father and husband they had lost. But at this stage Prince Philip found his son's timidity rather irritating. He had more in common with his fearless, outspoken daughter and though he would spank her when occasion demanded he really enjoyed the fact that she was not just 'the sweetest girl'.

The Queen's accession brought a change of home for her children, from familiar Clarence House to the vastness of Buckingham Palace. Of course they had stayed there many times while their parents were away but the Queen was nevertheless anxious about uprooting them and had her old nursery redecorated in exactly the same way as at Clarence House, to minimise the change. During the busy week the children only saw their parents for an hour or two every day but during the weekends at Windsor, and the holidays at Balmoral or Sandringham, the family were together a great deal.

For Prince Philip, his wife's new role brought personal problems of readjustment. During the previous four years he had been the unquestioned leader. 'Within the house and whatever we did, it was together. I suppose I naturally filled the principal position. People used to come to me and ask what to do.' When Elizabeth became Queen everyone felt it was their duty to go to her with plans, problems or ideas and Philip was bereft of a role. But the Queen made sure that in family matters he remained the head. This was not only in deference to his masculinity but because she felt his experience of the world was so much wider than hers. Whenever the children came to her with a problem she would reply 'Ask Papa, he'll know'. Although she frequently disagreed with him over the children's upbringing, particularly when it came to the

education of the heir, she always deferred to his judgment in the end.

Soon after Charles's fifth birthday his parents set off on the long tour of the Commonwealth which had been interrupted by the King's death. They were away for five months, which must have seemed an eternity to such young children, but care had been taken that the children understood the need for this separation. 'Mummy has an important job to do', Charles told a friend, and pointed out Australia on the globe: 'She's down here.' The Queen missed her children terribly. She kept their photos always beside her bed and sent off a stream of letters and postcards. On Christmas Day they spoke to her over the radio telephone from Sandringham. Before she left she had prepared their Christmas stockings; Prince Charles's included a velvet cloak and toy sword with which he played at coronations.

The Queen's return was the most exciting event in the children's lives so far. The royal yacht *Britannia* was equipped with a sandpit and a slide and carried the royal children out to Malta to spend a happy week with their great-uncle, Lord Mountbatten, before meeting their parents' ship at Tobruk. Princess Anne bounced up the

*April 1954: Prince Charles and Princess Anne on board the yacht* Britannia *just before she set sail from Portsmouth for Tobruk. They would be joining their parents there. Catherine Peebles and Helen Lightbody, the children's governess and nurse, accompanied the royal children.*

*Charles's first experience of school was afternoons playing football at Hill House in London.*

Peebles found Charles very nervous and sensitive. He was intelligent and interested but the mildest criticism hurt him dreadfully: 'If you raised your voice to him he would draw back into his shell and for a time you would be able to do nothing with him.' History, geography and painting were his favourite subjects but, like his mother, he had a blind spot for mathematics.

Two happy, protected years of childhood passed by in the Palace, then Prince Philip thought it was time to introduce his son to the more competitive environment of the outside world. He wanted Charles to go to boarding school and become tougher and more extrovert. The Queen and the Queen Mother were not at all happy with this idea. They fully appreciated the misery that a boy like Charles would feel away from home but they persuaded themselves that Prince Philip knew best. They did, however, insist that the change in his life was made as gradually as possible. First the supremacy of petticoat government was reduced when Nanny Lightbody was retired and a tutor appointed for his lessons. Then in the autumn of 1956 he was lowered gently into the shallow end by spending his afternoons playing football with the boys of Hill House school in Knightsbridge. After the New Year he began to attend full-time and the news of his emergence from the Palace awoke an appalling amount of press interest. On the third day of term the crowd of reporters and sightseers was so large that the Queen's press secretary had to ring round all the newspaper editors to get the press hounds recalled before Charles could make his way to school. At last, however, public interest died down and he settled, not unhappily, into the school routine. It was after all only a day school and by four o'clock he was back in the bosom of the family.

Setting off in September 1957 to a boarding school was a very different matter. As he travelled down from Balmoral with his mother, Charles shuddered at the prospect in store. He was bound for his father's old prep school, Cheam, near the Hampshire

gangplank saying hello to the sailors but Prince Charles behaved with his usual decorum. Indeed he politely stretched out a hand to his mother till she cried 'Oh, not you darling', and swept him into her arms. Reunited, the family set sail for England on board *Britannia*. It was a great homecoming; the royal yacht was cheered all the way to the Pool of London, then they transferred into a stately barge and glided upriver to a tumultuous welcome at Westminster pier.

With the excitement over and family life resumed, it was time for Prince Charles to begin proper lessons. He had already learned to ride and to dance, but now Miss Catherine Peebles was employed to lead him down more academic paths. After her previous pupils, Princess Alexandra and Prince Michael of Kent, Miss

Downs, where sixty-five acres of grounds would, it was hoped, shield him from prying eyes. Charles later remembered the few days after his arrival as the most miserable of his life. He stood in the playground, a forlorn solitary figure, unable to join in the games going on all around him. The other boys did not mean to be unkind but they were embarrassed to make overtures of friendship which might appear as if they were toadying. At night there was no privacy for tears in a dormitory of strangers. It seems unlikely that either George and Eddy joining *Britannia* or Edward and Bertie starting at Osborne suffered quite as much as this modern prince. Of course naval discipline was tougher than Cheam School but they had been twelve or thirteen when they left home, whereas Prince Charles was only eight.

To add to his problems, the interest of the press was remorseless. In his first term there were sixty-eight

*The Queen drives her children, near Windsor. Such informality is becoming increasingly rare, now that all members of the royal family are accompanied by bodyguards whenever they appear in public.*

*Princess Anne with her mother at Badminton Horse Trials in April 1960. At Anne's age Queen Elizabeth was a serious girl, the opposite of her boisterous, high-spirited daughter.*

stories about him in the newspapers; even the school barber was reported to be in the pay of some paper. During the Christmas holidays the Queen's press secretary held a meeting with Fleet Street editors and explained that so much harm was being done to the school that if it continued Prince Charles would have to return to Buckingham Palace, for the sake of his fellow schoolboys. Belatedly repentant the editors shifted the spotlight from Cheam and, apart from occasional invasions by foreign reporters, the school ran normally again.

Back at home Princess Anne was badgering her parents to let her go away to school but although she was much more confident than her brother they resisted her pleas for quite some while. Other little girls were brought

in to join her class but she tended to despise them on principle and they found her bossy and blunt. She had always preferred her mother's old rocking horse to any dolls and as soon as she began riding – at the age of three – it was obvious that she had an instinct for it. She combined the Queen's love for horses with the dash and daring her father displayed on the polo field. A favourite trick to shock the family was to gallop at a wall too high for her pony to jump and then slither to a standstill at the last moment. Such exhibitionism was not encouraged but a serious interest in riding certainly was. 'I've always tried to help them master at least one thing', Prince Philip has said, 'because as soon as a child feels self-confidence in one area, it spills over into all the others.' Under his guidance Anne also became a good swimmer and at nine years old was driving a bubble car along the private roads at Windsor. Due to Prince Philip's insistence she did not grow up in the neat kilts and pretty dresses which her mother had worn, but in hard-wearing trousers and sweaters. She made a delightful figure dressed up as a bridesmaid for her aunt's wedding but she had little interest in clothes or parties and much preferred mucking out the stables or sailing a dinghy with her father.

When Princess Anne was nine and Prince Charles eleven the Queen presented them with a baby brother: Andrew Albert Christian Edward. It is always assumed that this baby was part of a grand plan which had been suspended in the years immediately after the coronation because of pressure of work. But it is hard to believe the Queen had really planned to suffer the discomforts of early pregnancy during her seven weeks' visit to Canada in 1959. She insisted on keeping her condition secret so a host of other excuses had to be found for her loss of appetite and need for rest. By the end it was thought wiser to forego the scheduled sea trip and fly straight home to her doctors. 'I was glad indeed to feel that she was safely home', said the Prime Minister, Harold Macmillan, who would have preferred the Queen to cancel the trip.

The Queen went up to Balmoral to recuperate and gave up riding in favour of long walks across the moors. Prince Philip had bought a barbecue set in Canada and the family enjoyed using it on picnics in the hills. Princess Anne had a new bicycle that year and rode it everywhere. Unfortunately she once commissioned her father to ride it home for her from an outing and it buckled under his weight. There was a new face at Balmoral to interest the children; Tony Armstrong-Jones, their aunt's new romance, was invited to take a closer look at the royal family – and they of course looked closely at him. He lacked the necessary enthusiasm for outdoor activities to appeal to Prince Philip but to the children he was a breath of excitement from a different world. Here was an adult who numbered such fascinating personages as Harry Secombe and Peter Sellers among his friends!

Before Prince Andrew was born the Queen sorted out a tangle about the royal surname. On her marriage she had become theoretically a Mountbatten and it was felt that the Windsor name had to be legally reinstated. Prince Philip was furious: it made him just 'a bloody amoeba', he felt. After eight years on the throne the Queen had the confidence to put matters on a more equal footing with her husband, and eleven days before the birth she made this statement: 'The Queen has always wanted, without changing the name of the Royal House established by her grandfather, to associate the name of her husband with her own and his descendants. The Queen has had this in mind for a long time and it is close to her heart.' So while her House was still 'of Windsor' the family surname was henceforth Mountbatten-Windsor, and this appeared on Andrew's birth certificate a fortnight later.

The Queen was delighted to have another boy for she was anxious to protect Anne from being second in succession: 'I don't want her to have the life of my sister Margaret', she told a friend. From the outset Prince Andrew was a smiling, extrovert baby who grew into a lively and mischievous little boy. Nothing pleased him more than to tie together the laces on the boots of the Palace guardsmen or to hide 'whoopee' cushions among the armchairs. Another escapade was to climb on to the roof of Buckingham Palace and fiddle around with the aerials up there. Andrew could be stormy as well as fun – 'not always a little ray of sunshine', the Queen remarked – but he was a much more confident child than his elder brother and fitted more easily into his father's educational programme.

Soon after Andrew's birth Prince Charles moved on to the second leg of

*The Queen holds Prince Andrew, born 19 February 1960. She deliberately shielded her third child from publicity in his childhood years, and let him grow up in as normal an environment as possible.*

this programme, Gordonstoun school in north-east Scotland. Again it was his father's old school and though Charles thought it sounded 'pretty gruesome' he deferred to his father's wishes. 'My father had a particularly strong influence and it was good for me', he later recalled. 'I had perfect confidence in his judgment.' Given the sympathy the Queen and Duke felt for their children's problems it seems surprising that they encouraged their diffident son to go to a tough school where his extrovert father had been a great success. However, it was certainly a long way for reporters to travel, and he was possibly no more unhappy than he would have been anywhere else. A sensitive, private child, he can never have been really at ease in the public rough and tumble of a boarding school.

For royal children school life does not even offer the compensation of making lots of close friends. There is no child whose experience of life is quite like theirs, and they dare not exchange the confidences which are so essential to a growing friendship. Prince Philip once touched on the problem: 'The children soon discover that it's much safer to unburden yourself to a member of the family than just to a friend .... You see, you're never quite sure ... a small indiscretion can lead to all sorts of difficulties.'

Princess Anne was more fortunate than Prince Charles in her first experience of school because the system at Benenden, Kent, was for groups of girls to be looked after by an older 'house mother' and it was natural that she should make her first friends in this group. She described her circle as 'a caustic lot who knew exactly what they thought about other people and saved one a lot of embarrassment'. Although she had looked forward very much to going to school she discovered 'the amount of people and the noise was staggering'. Happy in her own company, this was one aspect of school which she found a constant trial. Like her elder brother she was trailed everywhere by a detective, who sometimes attracted more attention than she did. Once he was watching her at a riding lesson and his concentration caught the attention of men unloading a van. 'What's that man watching you for?' they enquired. 'You royalty or something?'

Anne put a lot of effort into school – not only academically, where she secured six O levels and two A levels – but into all that was going on. She played badminton, went swimming and rock climbing, sang in the choir, struggled with the oboe and acted in the Drama Club. But her chief enthusiasm was devoted to riding. Her pony High Jinks was stabled at a nearby riding school and they began to compete in gymkhanas. In 1968, the year she left school, Anne was given her first horse and was pleased to finish seventh in the novice class at the Windsor Horse Trials.

At Gordonstoun Charles was not faring as well. The conditions were spartan, the lessons demanding and the outdoor activities exhausting. He felt cut off from his family in the

*Prince Charles is shown around his father's old school Gordonstoun by Captain Iain Tennant of the Board of Governors. The headmaster, Mr Robert Chew, found himself having to mete out a punishment to the heir to the throne for the unfortunate Cherry Brandy incident.*

distant north and he was very homesick. And just as he was settling down
a little there was the dreadful embarrassment of the 'cherry brandy incident' in a Stornaway hotel. 'I thought
it was the end of the earth', he recollec-
ted later, 'I was all ready to pack my
bags and leave for Siberia.' The poor
boy had only slipped into the hotel bar
to avoid the stares of the public gazing
through the windows into the restau-
rant where he and his school party
were about to have a meal. Realising
that bars were for drinking in 'and
being terrified, not knowing what to
do I said the first drink which came
into my head, which happened to be
cherry brandy because I'd drunk it
before when it was cold, out shooting.
And hardly had I taken a sip when the
whole world exploded around my
ears.' Unfortunately a reporter was
lurking in the same hotel and the story
of a fourteen-year-old prince imbibing
alcohol under age was rapidly flashed
round the world. It was a tough lesson
to learn, that even in the remote Outer

*In June 1961 Princess
Anne was one of several
bridesmaids at the
wedding of the Duke of
Kent to Katharine Worsley
at York Minster. Yet she
was always happiest when
surrounded by horses, and
her great talent for riding
showed itself from a very
early age.*

Hebrides there were people keen to
publicise his slightest misdemeanour.

At the end of Charles's first term at
Gordonstoun there was a memorable
Christmas at Sandringham where four

*Andrew holds his infant baby brother, born 10 March 1964, in the music room at Buckingham Palace.*

of the royal ladies were pregnant. They made an imposing party setting out for a walk after lunch. In the evening there was a toast to 'all the little strangers we know are present'. First to make his appearance in 1964 was James Ogilvy, Princess Alexandra's first son, then came Prince Edward in March, then at the end of April Helen of Kent and Sarah Armstrong-Jones completed the quartet of cousins. Prince Edward was lucky enough, therefore, to have close relatives of his own age who shared his first lessons at Buckingham Palace and later some of his school experiences. Another occasional childhood companion was Lady Diana Spencer who lived at Park House on the Sandringham Estate.

The Queen was determined to enjoy her younger children and to protect them from publicity as much as possible. In fact so few photos were issued of Prince Andrew that the usual rumours suggested that there might be something wrong with him; the appearance of a plump healthy baby in the Queen's arms after the Trooping the Colour ceremony soon scotched that idea. The first real exposure the two youngest Princes received was when the television film *Royal Family* was shown to millions of people throughout the world. One of the most charming scenes was of the Queen sitting on a sofa between Andrew and Edward leafing through the family photo album. Seventy-five days of filming went into the programme, presenting a picture of family life which even the Prince Consort would have admired. Although the disadvantages of royal birth are great, the spacious homes of Sandringham, Balmoral, Windsor and Buckingham Palace offer enormous compensations to a sport-loving outdoor family like the present House of Windsor.

The Queen's children were devoted to both their parents, but they were also slightly in awe of them and were

*Above, the Queen and Princess Anne with Edward. Generally the Queen kept the young Edward well out of the limelight, but in 1968 she allowed a private photographic session at Frogmore, Windsor.*

*A still from* Royal Family: *the BBC film was a daring new departure for the family as well as for television. For the first time an ever-curious world was given a real taste of life for a royal child; and the Queen admitted cameras into her cherished private homes.*

## THE ROYAL FAMILY AT BALMORAL CASTLE

In September 1848 Queen Victoria fell in love with 'a pretty little castle in the old scotch style' on the banks of the River Dee near Ballater in Aberdeenshire. Yet scarcely had the royal family acquired it, for the sum of 30,000 guineas, than they decided it was too small for their ever-increasing family. In 1853 they laid the corner-stone of a new, much larger castle, and all the children signed a parchment that was buried underneath it; New Balmoral was to be their regular haven every autumn until the Queen's death. Opposite, right, Queen Victoria and the Prince of Wales welcome home a triumphant Albert with the stags, in a painting by C. Haag, 1854, (detail). When the Queen's favourite collie died in 1887 he was honoured with a memorial statue (opposite, left), one of many monuments still standing in the grounds.

Now the favourite royal dogs are corgis, and they enjoy their trips to Balmoral as well. Above, they join the royal family in a photocall marking the Queen's 32nd wedding anniversary; Peter Phillips was there too (far left).

Balmoral is a greatly treasured retreat from the rigours of public life for the

present royal family. Every year they go northwards as the heather comes into bloom, and spend several relaxed weeks shooting, hunting, fishing and walking in the lochs and mountains of Deeside. Above, Princess Anne cooks a barbecue with her father in the grounds. It is a very private home, and glimpses inside (right, of the Queen and Prince Philip), are very rare. Crathie Church is their place of worship while in residence.

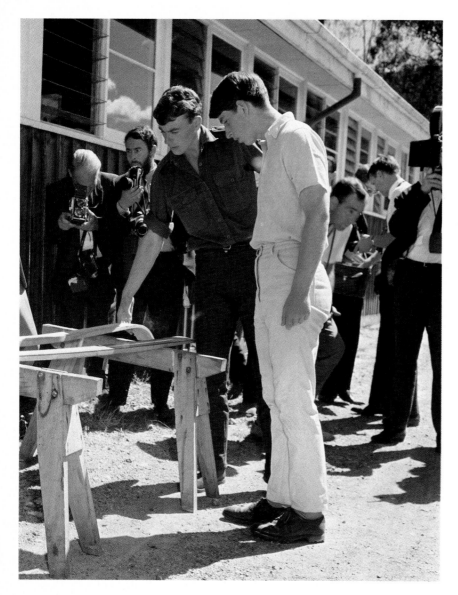

*Opposite:*

*Prince Charles at Timbertop. Looking back, he sees what a formative experience it was for him: 'In Australia you are judged on how people see you and feel about you. There are no assumptions. You have to fend for yourself.'*

*Opposite: another turning-point in Charles's life was his investiture as Prince of Wales at Caernarvon Castle in 1969. Kneeling before his mother he took the oath of allegiance to the sovereign, for which he had been considered too young at her coronation.*

things. For me she has been one of those extraordinarily rare people whose touch can turn everything to gold.'

Towards the end of his time at Gordonstoun Prince Charles began to find his feet. He passed six O levels, developed an interest in archaeology, learned the cello and starred in Macbeth. But it was two terms in Australia, 'the most wonderful experience I've ever had', that really gave him confidence and maturity. The transformation was wrought by Timbertop, an outpost of Geelong School, which was even tougher than Gordonstoun in its physical demands but had a much more relaxed atmosphere. The boys were interested in the Prince, but quite unawed, and after only a few days he felt at home. 'Australia conquered my shyness', he later said. Back at Gordonstoun the last year passed pleasantly enough but he had outgrown school by now and in 1967 he was delighted to exchange the northern wastes for the tranquillity and civilisation of Trinity College, Cambridge.

His three years as an undergraduate were interrupted by a term at Aberystwyth University to learn Welsh before his investiture as Prince of Wales at Caernarvon Castle. The Welsh Nationalists strongly objected to his presence and there were fears for his safety but his quiet charm and dedication soon won them over. 'He came and saw and conquered the Welsh', Prince Philip remarked proudly. And great too was the Queen's pride when she presented her eldest son to the Welsh people. For him it was the end of childhood and the beginning of public life.

Princess Anne was now also becoming a public figure. She had left Benenden in 1968 with no clear idea of what to do next, except to carry on with her riding. Her parents were not sure this would prove fulfilling for long but the Princess' success – she was voted Sportswoman of the Year in 1971 – delighted them. They were pleased too when through her interest in horses she met and married Mark

lucky to be able also to confide in a wonderful grandmother and an 'honorary grandfather'. The 'grandfather' was actually their father's uncle, Lord Mountbatten, who was a particularly strong influence on Prince Charles until his tragic assassination in 1979. Queen Elizabeth the Queen Mother was the ideal loving, admiring, listening grandmother who rarely criticised but always encouraged. It was she who convinced Charles he must stick it out at Gordonstoun in the first, most unhappy term, and she also took her helicopter into Benenden so that she could visit Princess Anne. In 1979 Prince Charles wrote of her: 'Ever since I can remember my grandmother has been the most wonderful example of fun, laughter, warmth, infinite security and, above all else, exquisite taste in so many

*The royal family photographed at Balmoral at the time of the celebrations for the Queen's Silver Wedding in 1972. Not long afterwards Anne was to be the first to leave the security of the family for marriage to Captain Mark Phillips.*

Phillips. With the unfortunate experiences of Princess Margaret in mind they were desperately anxious that their only daughter should choose the right man.

Andrew and Edward were growing up with many fewer problems than their elders. Andrew was polite or aggressive, diligent or idle, as the mood took him, but he bounced through Cheam and into Gordonstoun with none of the anguish of his elder brother. Edward, whom the Queen has called 'the quietest of my children', was not as confident as Andrew but more self-contained than Charles, and without the anxiety to fulfil expectations which has always tended to trouble the heir to the throne. Prince Edward had the reassuring company of his second cousin James Ogilvy at his prep school, Heatherdown, and by the time he reached Gordonstoun Andrew was already a senior boy and

able to smooth his path a little.

Gordonstoun had changed considerably since Prince Charles's time. A new headmaster believed in central heating and a warm swimming pool and co-education. With the arrival of girl students social life became very good indeed and both Princes have had a chance to meet women in a much more natural way than their eldest brother. Prince Andrew arrived at Gordonstoun rather full of himself but the good-natured teasing of his fellows soon brought him down to earth. However, it cannot have hurt his ego to be fetched in a royal plane to attend his sister's wedding in the November of his first term. Prince Edward was a charming kilted page-boy with just one bridesmaid, his cousin Sarah, as Princess Anne didn't want the occasion spoiled by 'hordes of children' running around.

Back at Gordonstoun Prince

*Prince Edward and his cousin Lady Sarah Armstrong-Jones were the only two attendants at Princess Anne's wedding.*

Andrew developed into 'a very tough and independent young fellow', as one of the masters said. 'He has no time for sycophants. On the other hand, if anyone tries to take the mickey out of him he doesn't hesitate to fight back. He's good – just as good – with verbalistics as he is with his fists.' In 1977 he spent two terms at Lakefield College – the Canadian equivalent of Timbertop – which proved a broadening experience and rubbed off some of his aggressive corners. He returned to Gordonstoun and passed three A levels but went straight into the Navy on a twelve-year commission rather than to university. Fortunately this traditional career for royal princes is well suited to Andrew's energetic and vigorous temperament. He trained as a helicopter pilot and, to everyone's surprise and dismay, had the same opportunity to prove himself in battle as his father in World War II and his grandfather

George VI at the Battle of Jutland. In 1982 he sailed with the Task Force on the carrier HMS *Invincible* to the Falkland Islands, and remained there on duty for several months after the war had ended.

Since Prince Edward has always been considered the quietest and most contemplative of the Queen's children, it was suggested that he might escape a service career and follow the Duke of Gloucester's example in taking up one of the professions. However, as he emerges from the privacy of a sheltered childhood his serene image has been rather shattered by indignant clashes with the press and a tough training stint with the Marines, which he will probably join after finishing three years at Jesus College, Cambridge. Looking back on the Gordonstoun years, he remarked: 'I think, whatever you're doing, a school is a school and I don't agree with the statement that

*Edward with his young cousin, Lady Rose Victoria Birgitte Louise, on the occasion of her christening, 13 July 1980 (see also page 99). Both he and Lady Sarah Armstrong-Jones are among the godparents. Below, his elder brother Andrew arrives back from the Falklands, several months after the end of the conflict.*

schooldays are the happiest days of your life. Although I will admit that my last term at Gordonstoun was probably the most enjoyable. As Head Boy I was doing and learning a lot . . .'

Like his elder brothers he thoroughly enjoyed some time elsewhere: in his case it was the Collegiate School, Wanganui in New Zealand, but as he had already taken A levels he went as a teacher, not a student. 'What I like most about New Zealand', he said, 'is the friendliness. It hit me when I first came here. It may be partly because people emigrated here, and it was sparsely populated, and they always wanted to know their neighbours. It's probably a hangover from that and it makes life better.'

Looking at their two eldest children, happily embarked upon parenthood, and their two youngest set fair for rewarding careers, the Queen and Prince Philip must feel great satisfaction and relief that the difficult childhood years are over. It is so easy to overdo simplicity – like giving Charles the smallest toy boat on the Cheam pond – or to push too hard: 'The trouble is, everyone expects one to be a genius' he once said. But although there have been mistakes and misunderstandings, the love and security of the home background has always been the staunchest support to the Queen's children. Princess Anne said in 1980: 'The greatest advantage of my entire life is the family I grew up in. I'm eternally thankful for being able to grow up in the sort of atmosphere that was given to me . . . the family was always there, the feeling of being in a family, and we are the stronger for it I think.'

*The Queen Mother celebrates her 83rd birthday. With her outside Clarence House are her two daughters (Princess Margaret is to her right), her favourite grandson Charles, Princess Diana and Lady Sarah Armstrong-Jones. Such opportunities for the family to be together are treasured moments of the royal calendar.*

# 5

# ROYAL COUSINS

'I shall soon have a regiment, not a family', boasted George v long ago, and how proud he would be today to see the massed battalions of his descendants who grace every royal occasion. For although his eldest son, the Duke of Windsor, had no children, and his youngest died in adolescence, the four remaining children were fruitful and multiplied. From his second son George VI descend the Queen's family and Princess Margaret's children; from his daughter Mary, Princess Royal, come the Harewood family; from Prince Henry and Prince George descend the Gloucesters and the Kents.

The most senior of the royal cousins is Prince Richard, Duke of Gloucester, but he is so much younger than the Queen that it is often forgotten that they are in fact first cousins. Prince Richard's father Henry married Lady Alice Montagu-Douglas-Scott late in life, and she was almost forty before her first son, William, was born in 1941. Soon after the birth Prince Henry was sent to Scotland on service with the Army and Queen Mary commiserated with Princess Alice on his absence: 'What a pity Harry will miss three months of the baby's adorable baby days which one simply loves, especially the first one! You cannot think how Papa enjoyed our first baby (that naughty boy!!!) he was always in and out of the nursery.'

William was an outward-going, lively infant, usually covered in bruises because his inquisitive nature led him to climb on anything and everything in too great a hurry. When he was three a baby brother was born, to the great delight of Queen Mary. 'What joy! another boy. I am enchanted. I hope this time you will call him Richard which sounds so well with Gloucester.' She must have forgotten that an earlier Richard of Gloucester was the wicked uncle of the Princes in the Tower! Prince Henry was not keen on the name because, his wife said, 'he can never pronounce the letter R', but in the end the Queen won the day.

A few months later both little Princes set sail for Australia where their father was to be Governor General. It was still wartime and they had a hazardous journey avoiding U boats. Tins of baby food for Richard were carried on two ships in case one of them was sunk. At the end of January 1945 they arrived on the other side of the world and Prince William enjoyed the first orange he had ever seen. Like his namesake Prince William of Wales in 1983, he was the star attraction wherever the Gloucesters went. 'William the Conqueror, the travelling salesman of Britain', he was called in

*Lady Sarah Armstrong-Jones (far left) and the Queen greet the dogs. On the Queen's left are the Duke of Beaufort, Princess Margaret, Viscount Linley and the Duchess of Beaufort.*

*Members of the royal family appear on the steps of St George's Chapel, Windsor. From left to right: Princess Michael of Kent, Lady Sarah Armstrong-Jones, Princess Margaret, the Dowager Duchess of Gloucester, and the Duchess of Gloucester. Behind her is Lady Helen Windsor, and to her right her brother, the Earl of St Andrews.*

*The Australian Woman's Weekly.* He was a very sociable child and often broke the ice at official functions with his uninhibited behaviour. Once, at the age of three, he offered to introduce a large lady to someone the other side of a crowded room. After a few moments unsuccessfully pushing he said: 'I'm very sorry, we'll have to go round by the corridor. You're too fat.'

Although there were some memorable tours and events the Gloucesters found the climate and conditions in Australia rather trying and they all suffered most unfortunate bouts of ill-health. After two years they were summoned home to hold the fort while George VI and his family made a lengthy tour of South Africa. They remained in England, living chiefly at Barnwell Manor near Peterborough, but also renting for Scottish holidays the House of Farr in Invernesshire. It was here, walking, riding and hunting, that they enjoyed, as the Duchess said, 'the happiest days of all'.

Every year they spent one week at Balmoral, playing with their numerous cousins. Prince Richard was very taken aback one day when Princess Anne, only five or six years old, rushed into his room one morning, seized his dagger and thrust it through the eiderdown into the mattress, exclaiming

'I've always wanted to do this'. The Duchess suggested her son should have reported the matter in case he was blamed for the damage but he shook his head: 'No, I couldn't tell on her.'

The Gloucester Princes were brought up with as little fuss and formality as possible. Both went to Wellesley House at Broadstairs, then to Eton and Cambridge. William was the bouncy and adventurous one. 'He was always such a restless, active person', his mother recalled, 'that I have often wondered if he had some premonition that his life was to be short.' In 1972 he was killed in a flying accident while taking part in an air race near Wolverhampton. 'I was completely stunned', wrote the Duchess, 'and have never been quite the same since, though I have tried to persuade myself that it was better to have known and lost him than never to have had him at all.'

Prince Richard had always been a quiet, observant rather lazy child, full of admiration for his brother and rather overshadowed by him. It was William who had noticed how clever Richard was at making models and suggested that he should read architecture at Cambridge. This proved a great success both professionally and personally, for Richard not only found something he was really good at, but also met his future wife Birgitte van Deurs, daughter of a Danish lawyer, who had been studying at a Cambridge language school. They were married in July 1972.

Prince Richard and Birgitte began married life in a terraced house in Camden Town and looked forward to the pleasant, private existence of a professional family in London. But two deaths in two years shattered their plans. Only a month after their wedding the tragic loss of Prince William made Richard heir to the dukedom and two years later his father died after a long and sad illness. Suddenly they found themselves Duke and Duchess of Gloucester, with apartments in Kensington Palace and an

*Prince William of Gloucester as a baby with his father Prince Henry in 1943.*

endless round of public duties. Sadly the old Duke had died four months before the birth of his first grandchild, Alexander, Earl of Ulster. The Duchess had already had one miscarriage and with her second pregnancy went into premature labour at seven months. However the baby was safely delivered by Caesarian section and rapidly grew into a strong and handsome child. Two sisters were born in 1977 and 1980; first came Lady Davina and then Lady Rose, who was carried to her christening at Barnwell Church in a pony and trap laden with flowers and driven by her proud father. The Duke of Gloucester maintained his architectural practice for many years but eventually the combined pressures of royal engagements, farming at Barnwell, and family life forced him to relinquish his partnership.

The young Gloucesters are growing up in the happiest of circumstances. In London they slide down the banisters of Kensington Palace and in the country they have a playground of 2,500 acres around Barnwell Manor. Although both their parents lead active and interesting lives, family life is the central focus and the Duke will hurry back from an official lunch to collect his son from school. Far enough from the throne to escape the harshest spotlight of public interest

*Richard, the present Duke of Gloucester, and his family at the christening of his youngest daughter.*

*Opposite: Prince William explores the jet boat* Crusader *with his brother Richard (left), 1952.*

and criticism, the Gloucesters are nonetheless great-grandchildren of George V and share all the fun of royal gatherings at Sandringham, Balmoral and Windsor. They can look forward to a relaxed childhood and their own choice of career, as well as the occasional magic of a great royal occasion.

Whereas Prince Richard was thirty when he took up the duties of Duke of Gloucester, his cousin Edward was only six when the death of his father made him Duke of Kent. Prince George had been the youngest surviving child of King George and Queen Mary, and was his mother's favourite son because of his outgoing nature and interest in art and music. He married Princess Marina of Greece and Denmark in 1934 and they had three children: Edward, born in 1935, Alexandra in 1936 and Michael in 1942. Although it was a love match the Duke found it hard at first to settle into the routine of family life after his jolly bachelor existence and Princess Marina chafed at some of the restrictions of English royal life. She was not prepared to be completely dominated by her husband's wishes, as Queen Mary had been with George V. But they both adored the children and their personalities mellowed in the enjoyment of family life. The Duke was particularly delighted when his elder son showed a great interest in machinery and they would spend hours in the garage together tinkering with cars.

In the early part of the war Edward and Alexandra were sent to stay with their grandmother, Queen Mary, at Badminton in Gloucestershire and saw little of their parents, but a protective steel roof was erected over the day nursery at Coppins, their country home, and in 1941 the family was reunited again. Prince Michael of Kent was born there in July 1942 and given Franklin as his fourth name in honour of President Roosevelt, a godfather. The Duke made a great fuss of his third child, as the visiting Baroness de Stoeckl noted in her diary:

> Every evening instead of sitting late as usual, he leaves the table shortly after 10 o'clock and carries his youngest son to the nursery and lays him on his cot and stands watching and watching. Nanny told me that each night as he lays his son in his cot she discreetly leaves the room but she can hear the Duke talking softly to him.

Sadly, it is only through accounts like this that Prince Michael can know how much his father loved him for

when he was seven weeks old the Duke was killed in a flying accident on active service in Scotland.

Princess Marina was devastated and only the needs of her young baby and the sympathy and support of the whole royal family enabled her to carry on. Apart from the grief and loneliness of her position she was troubled with financial problems as her husband's Civil List annuity ceased on his death. Although Princess Alexandra was embarrassed to be photographed in clothes which had been worn by her cousins Princess Elizabeth and Princess Margaret, she was not at that stage particularly interested in her appearance. The elegant, gracious and charming Princess of today was a restless, temperamental tomboy, very like the young Princess Anne. Perhaps it was because they

*Princess Marina, Duchess of Kent, holds the present Duke's hand as they leave Belgrave Square for a holiday at Sandwich in July 1937. The baby Alexandra looks very surprised about something.*

both had elder brothers who tended to draw the limelight.

Princess Alexandra had spent a large part of the war years with Queen Mary but even that very proper old lady could not repress her high spirits. A visitor noticed, 'She got on admirably with her grandmother Queen Mary, who was at moments taken aback by her energy, but fascinated too, and who bore her granddaughter's exuberance with amused fortitude'. The Princess was educated locally at first, then became the first member of the royal family to go to a boarding school, Heathfield near Ascot. She enjoyed school but her chief gift, inherited from her father, was for playing the piano. After being 'finished' in France she emerged from the gawky teenage years as a well-dressed, confident young woman, one of the

most popular in the royal league.

During her early twenties Alexandra's name was romantically linked with several royal houses, but she surprised everyone in 1963 by marrying a reserved Scottish businessman, Angus Ogilvy, second son of the Earl of Airlie. They live at Thatched House Lodge in Richmond with their two children, James, born in 1964 and Marina, 1966. Angus Ogilvy made it clear from the start that he was not going to trail behind his wife at every engagement but would pursue his own business interests. This has helped to make the marriage a very happy one, but he has not been able to escape altogether the pressures of a royal marriage. Back in 1971 he explained the dilemma of public life:

I think the time is coming very shortly when if we don't see a lot more of our

*Queen Mary chats with two of her grandsons during an official royal visit to the South Bank Festival site in 1951. Prince Michael of Kent is to the right, and Prince William of Gloucester to the left.*

*Princess Alexandra with Angus Ogilvy, Marina and James. Both children were born at their present home, Thatched House Lodge in the royal park of Richmond; tall bushes keep out both the deer and curious members of the public. Right: James Ogilvy with his father. He and his sister are both good pianists, and he is also interested in photography, art and architecture. Below: Marina hauls herself out of the water and gets back to windsurfing at Cowes.*

children, we're going to pay the price at the other end, when they're older. But it's very difficult. You decide to spend an evening with the children, but then someone rings up and says 'Will you please come to a film premier. If you come it will help us raise another £1,500 and this could help, say, 300 spastics'. Well, who are more important, 300 spastics, or your own children?

James Ogilvy is only a month older than Prince Edward and for a while they shared lessons at Buckingham Palace. Then James went on to Gibbs School, Heatherdown and to Eton. After passing thirteen O levels and three A levels he went to St Andrews University in Scotland in the autumn of 1983. His sister Marina leaves St Mary's school in Wantage in 1984 and her next step is not yet known. Her special interests are music and dancing; as a young girl she was a great lover of horses, but, unlike Princess Anne, that fascination has not stood the test of time.

*George, Earl of St Andrews, considered the cleverest of all the royal cousins.*

Princess Marina had been mildly disappointed at Princess Alexandra's choice of a husband for, much as she liked Angus Ogilvy, she had hoped that one of her children would make a royal marriage, and her eldest son had already married a commoner, Katharine Worsley. After going to Eton the young Duke of Kent joined the Army, and when his regiment was posted to Catterick in 1956 he was among the young officers entertained at nearby Hovingham Hall by Sir William Worsley. He was only twenty-one, with a reputation for fast driving and high living, but he soon became devotedly attached to Sir William's daughter Katharine. She was two years older than he and, though Princess Marina had to admit: 'She is a

*Lady Helen Windsor, daughter of the Duke of Kent, photographed by Snowdon for her 18th birthday, 28 April 1982. She was born in the same year as James Ogilvy, Prince Edward and Lady Sarah Armstrong-Jones.*

pretty, sweet person', she felt – indeed hoped – that the Duke was too young to know his own mind. On his father's side he could trace his ancestry back to William I, on her side to Charlemagne, and Princess Marina would have loved to see her son make a royal alliance worthy of such ancestors. When the Duke wanted to marry in 1958, before being posted to Germany, consent was refused and it was not until 1961 that the wedding eventually took place. Once convinced of her son's steadfast feelings for Katharine, however, Princess Marina warmly welcomed her into the family and took a great delight in her three grandchildren.

George, Earl of St Andrews, was born in 1962 and at only five months he travelled with his parents to an Army posting in Hong Kong. In 1964 came a daughter, Lady Helen, and the four Kents decamped to Germany to spend eighteen months in married quarters. In 1970 a second son, Lord Nicholas Windsor, completed the family, and when he was three they moved from Coppins to Anmer Hall, a large house in a 10-acre park on the Sandringham estate.

The Earl of St Andrews was a sweet little boy, with curly hair and an angelic expression, very much in demand as a page-boy. At first he was sent to the local day-school, Eton End, Datchet, and from there to Heatherdown following in the steps of Prince Andrew and Prince Edward. He was the first member of the royal family to

*Lord Nicholas, also by Snowdon. Lady Helen's younger brother, he has a great interest in music, and at the age of 10 set a new royal precedent by appearing at Covent Garden in Mozart's* Magic Flute.

win a scholarship, a prestigious King's Scholarship to Eton. Although he unexpectedly failed two of his three A levels at the first attempt, he retook them successfully and won a place at Downing College, Cambridge, in the autumn of 1982 to study history. Lady Helen went to St Paul's preparatory school in London then to St Mary's Wantage. For her A levels she moved to Gordonstoun, and she is now working in an art gallery. Lord Nicholas Windsor attends Westminster School in London.

The Kent and Ogilvy children have recently acquired some new, much younger cousins after the marriage of their uncle Prince Michael to Baroness Marie-Christine von Reibnitz. Six years younger than his sister Princess Alexandra, Prince Michael never knew his father but he was his mother's darling. He was very fortunate in his governess, Miss Catherine Peebles, who did not spoil him, although she was a great favourite and went on to Buckingham Palace to

*Edward, Duke of Kent, skiing with his youngest son in Switzerland: it is a sport that the families of the Dukes of Kent and of Gloucester greatly enjoy. Below, his wife and Lady Helen at the Sandringham Flower Show.*

begin the education of Prince Charles and Princess Anne. At five years old Prince Michael was a train-bearer to his first cousin Princess Elizabeth at her wedding to Prince Philip in 1947. During the ceremony he and William of Gloucester behaved admirably but later on, Marion Crawford remembered, they 'were thoroughly overtired, grew peevish and almost came to blows. Shocked nannies enveloped them in those vast white shawls royal nannies always seem to have handy. Like sheltering wings! They were borne off, but not before they had made ceremonious bows to the King and Queen. In royal circles manners are taught young.'

Prince Michael of Kent was an eligible bachelor for many years but when he did fall in love he was not deterred by the fact that his fiancée was a divorced Roman Catholic Austrian, Baroness Marie-Christine von Reibnitz. The Baroness was very anxious to obtain a papal dispensation allowing her to be married by the Church but this fell through because

Prince Michael could not agree to the children being brought up as Roman Catholics. The 1701 Act of Succession ensures that no one in line of succession to the throne can marry a Catholic; Prince Michael renounced his right for himself but not for his children, who therefore must be raised in the Church of England. It was a great disappointment for the Baroness as plans for a wedding at the Schottenkirche in Vienna had to be switched to the town hall. However, the marriage was blessed at a private mass the following morning, and the Queen's personal approval was conferred by the granting of the title 'Royal Highness' which had been so much desired by the Duchess of Windsor. Princess Michael has adapted easily to royal life and carries out her engagements with zest and style. Lord Frederick Windsor, born in 1979, attends Wetherby school in London and Lady Gabriella, born in 1981, is still in the nursery. The children's country home is Nether Lypiatt Manor, near Stroud in Gloucestershire.

*Prince and Princess Michael of Kent with Lord Frederick and his little sister Lady Gabriella, born 23 April 1981. Technically the children remain in the line of succession, although their father has renounced his own place.*

*Princess Margaret, Lord Snowdon and their young family, photographed by Cecil Beaton. Even at this early stage the relationship was showing signs of strain.*

Two royal cousins whose childhood has been much saddened by the shadow of divorce are of course David, Viscount Linley and Lady Sarah Armstrong-Jones. When Princess Margaret's first great romance with Peter Townsend came to an end because, though the innocent party in a divorce case, he was not considered a fitting match for the Queen's sister, many people felt the Princess had been badly treated by the Church and the press. So a particular warmth and sympathy went out to her when six years after renouncing Townsend she was married to Antony Armstrong-Jones, a fashionable photographer, in Westminster Abbey. All the world hoped that this talented, vivacious twenty-nine-year-old had found happiness at last, but some of those close to her had grave doubts. They feared that

Margaret and Tony were too alike, both stubborn and self-willed and perhaps self-centred, and that neither would be good at the tolerance and compromise essential for a lasting marriage.

At first, however, they were thoroughly enchanted with each other and in 1961 their son David was born into a home of wit, gaiety and laughter. But even young David brought problems with him, for in order to please the Queen, who thought her nephew should not go untitled, Tony agreed to become Earl of Snowdon a few months before David's birth. His son automatically took on the subsidiary title of Viscount Linley. The acceptance of an earldom aroused a lot of carping criticism in the press which a proud independent man like Snowdon found hard to bear. And although

his royal in-laws encouraged him to pursue his artistic interests, there were still many formal occasions on which he had to accompany his wife – a step behind. By the time of Princess Margaret's second pregnancy his discontent was affecting their relationship to such an extent that her doctors feared for her health. The birth of Lady Sarah Frances Elizabeth in 1964 brought them closer for a little while, and they planted a red climbing rose in their Kensington Palace garden to mark the occasion. But the children did not hold them together for long. By 1966, as Christopher Warwick writes in his recent biography: 'He had withdrawn his support and was destroying the peace and harmony of their home life which Princess Margaret felt acutely. In many ways it was as though she were now married to a stranger.'

This cannot have been a happy environment for the children to grow up in. Even on family holidays their father could descend into unpredictable black moods. In 1973 all four of them were holidaying in Italy and they had scarcely arrived when Lord Snowdon fell into a long silence. 'Papa,

*Lady Sarah Armstrong-Jones, above with her brother at Badminton House, and below with her ice lolly.*

*Lady Sarah goes to college. Both she and her brother Viscount Linley (below) have great artistic gifts, inherited from two talented parents.*

Mummy is talking to you', said one of the children. 'I know', is all he replied. After a week he abandoned them all and returned to London alone.

When David was fourteen and Sarah eleven Lord Snowdon finally moved out of Kensington Palace and a formal separation was agreed. Princess Margaret retained custody of the children but their father was to have free access. Commenting on the official statement of the separation he made a special plea 'for the understanding of our two children'.

Originally Lord Linley was destined to follow his father to Eton but he was not gifted academically and the more sensible choice was made of Bedales, a co-educational boarding school.

(When Lord Snowdon was at Eton one report had read: 'Maybe he is interested in some subject, but it isn't a subject we teach here'.) Lord Linley's talent proved to be in craftwork, especially carpentry, and he went from Bedales to the John Makepeace School for Craftsmen at Parnham in Dorset. The Monday after leaving school he started work with two friends making furniture in workshops at Dorking: 'We had the rent to pay. We had to start making money as soon as possible ... I am entirely self-financed.'

Lady Sarah also went to Bedales and showed a talent for art and craft. Although she accompanied her mother on an official visit to Canada in 1981 there has been no suggestion that either child should play a royal role in future. 'My children are not royal,' Princess Margaret has said, 'they just happen to have an aunt who is Queen.'

And yet their closeness to their cousins, Charles, Anne, Andrew and Edward is undeniable, shown, for example, by the choice of Lady Sarah as chief or only bridesmaid in both the royal weddings. Perhaps the service of thanksgiving at the Silver Jubilee best sums up their dual status: they rode in an open carriage with their mother to St Paul's but while the rest of the royal family went on to lunch at the Guildhall, Lord Snowdon collected them for a quiet meal elsewhere. It cannot be easy to switch from one life to the other in this way but it is fortunate that both children have artistic gifts which will enable them to carve out their own positions in society. In 1982 Lady Sarah gained a much-coveted place in Camberwell School of Art in London, so despite the disappointment of their marriage Princess Margaret and Lord Snowdon must take a great pride and pleasure in their children.

*Prince Edward and Lady Sarah, always a close friend of her cousins at the Palace, watch Prince Charles play polo for England at Windsor.*

# 6

# THE NEW GENERATION

All the Queen's children had been born in Buckingham Palace but the trend against home births changed even the traditions of the royal family. The Queen's first grandson was born to Princess Anne in the private wing of St Mary's Hospital, Paddington, under the care of Mr George Pinker, Surgeon Gynaecologist to the Queen.

The Princess had been glad there was no pressure on her to rush into motherhood: 'It's not a duty', she said, 'because I'm not a boy'. Unlike most royal mothers Princess Anne enjoyed three years of married life, pursuing horse and country interests with her husband Mark before she became pregnant. And even then, though she soon gave up riding, she accompanied Mark to shows and competitions, unconcerned about her bulging shape. It set a new style of 'open' pregnancy which the Princess of Wales was quick to follow. Previously royal ladies had

*Princess Anne with baby Peter, photographed by Lord Snowdon in August 1978.*

been very seldom seen in public once their condition had been announced.

Princess Anne hoped the baby would arrive on her fourth wedding anniversary but it was on the following day, 15 November 1977, that a healthy 7lb 9oz boy made his appearance. The Queen was at Buckingham Palace preparing for an investiture when Princess Anne herself rang through with the news. It made the Queen ten minutes late, but who could object when she walked in wreathed in smiles and announced 'My daughter has just given birth to a son'. She had always hoped for a grandchild 'while I'm young enough to enjoy being a grandmother', and she drove to the hospital that evening looking radiantly happy. The baby's other grandparents were delighted as

*Right: Peter with his
parents, 15 August 1980.*

*Left: Peter Phillips as a
page-boy at the wedding of
his aunt Sarah Phillips.*

well and at the Phillips' home reporters were invited to toast 'the little one
as yet unnamed'.

A week later he was christened
Peter Mark Andrew in the Music
Room at Buckingham Palace. Heading
the five generations present was Princess Alice, Countess of Athlone, the
last surviving grandchild of Queen
Victoria, who had herself been christened from the same gold font under
the eagle eye of the old Queen, ninety-
four years before.

Although the Queen had offered
Mark Phillips a title he preferred to
remain a commoner and so his son,
though so close to the throne, is plain
Master Phillips. Mark and Anne

were nevertheless delighted to accept
the Queen's gift of Gatcombe Park
in Gloucestershire. The pleasant,
spacious eighteenth-century mansion
stands in the middle of a 730-acre
estate with a separate 500-acre farm
adjoining. Captain Phillips' Army
career was hampered by the impossi-
bility of his serving in Northern
Ireland and so he sensibly faced facts
and retrained at agricultural college.
Now he can test out the theories on his
own farm and share with Princess
Anne the interest – and business – of
breeding horses. It will be a relaxed
country upbringing for Peter and
Zara, born in May 1981.

Princess Anne describes herself as

*Princess Anne's children will be able to escape from many of the formal royal obligations that restricted her own life when she was a child. Left, she holds her daughter Zara, also pictured below, while Peter holds on to their bodyguard's ears at the Windsor Horse Show. He is also pictured opposite.*

'not particularly maternal in outlook' but her delight in her children is obvious and Peter is already an entertaining companion at sporting events. The Queen, too, has found great pleasure in giving him his first riding lessons and strolling hand in hand with him round the Windsor Horse Show. Princess Anne is going to enjoy exactly the lifestyle which the Queen always wanted – 'in the country with lots of horses and dogs' – and there can be no doubt that in future years the Queen will find great relaxation visiting her daughter's family. Prince Philip is not the sort of man to make a great fuss of babies but as Peter grows into a sturdy long-limbed boy his grandfather will enjoy introducing him to all the sports he taught his own children. Already he has looked out the mini-caravan in which Charles and Anne used to be pulled around the grounds and has had it restored as a present for Peter.

The nursery at Gatcombe Park was first presided over by Mabel Anderson, who had been nanny to Princess Anne, but she left in 1981 and was replaced by Pat Moss. The household is friendly and informal, with its staff limited to a

butler, a cook, a dresser and two cleaning ladies. It is fortunate that Mark works on the estate for when Princess Anne is away on royal engagements he is free to run Peter to the village school and to read a bedtime story to Zara. Princess Anne still works very hard at the royal round. She is an active patron of many good causes and makes overseas trips to forward the work of the Save the Children Fund. She does not feel, however, that this role will be carried on in her branch of the family: 'I doubt if the next generation will be involved at all', she has said. Like Viscount Linley and Lady Sarah, the Phillips children will be free to make their own way in the world, unhindered by the penalties of royal birth.

The fate of their first cousin, Prince William of Wales, is of course very different. Eldest son of an eldest son, he is born to be king, and only abdication or revolution will change his destiny.

His birth on 21 June 1982 was the crowning glory of a wonderful two years for Prince Charles and Lady Diana. In June 1980 she was one of many pretty young girls from wealthy families who share London flats and find pleasant jobs to occupy themselves until Prince Charming comes along. Even daydreaming about the future together, as young flatmates do, she could never have guessed that two years later she would be mother of a future king of Great Britain.

Her family had always had many connections with the royal family and Diana grew up in Park House near Sandringham, but it was Prince Andrew who was closest in age to her whereas Prince Charles had at one time courted her elder sister Sarah. In fact it was when staying at the Spencer home of Althorp as a guest of Lady Sarah in 1977 that he first took notice of her youngest sister, 'a splendid 16-year-old', who was growing up fast.

Lady Diana left school that year and

*A nursery for a modern Prince: the Princess of Wales chose this furniture for William's rooms at Kensington Palace.*

went in January 1978 to a finishing school in Switzerland. Her French teacher recalled that she 'was very idealistic about what she wanted for herself. She knew she wanted to work with children – and then she wanted to get married and have children of her own'. When she came back in March for the wedding of her sister Jane she decided not to return to the Continent but to get a job as a nanny straight away. She enjoyed the work very much but when in the summer of 1979 her parents bought her a three-bedroomed flat in Brompton Road to share with friends she decided to take a position with more regular hours at a local private kindergarten.

She had met Prince Charles again several times since the Althorp visit but it was in the autumn of 1979, on a visit to the Queen Mother at Birkhall near Balmoral, that they really became aware of each other. Walking, picnicking and fishing together in the Scottish hills they gradually discovered, as Prince Charles put it, that 'there was something in it'. Unfortunately the world's press were not far behind this new development and as soon as Lady Diana returned to her job in London she was hounded by reporters. When she was invited to visit Sandringham during the Christmas holidays press attention was so relentless that Prince Charles was driven to wish reporters 'a happy New Year and your editors a particularly nasty one'.

In fact it was to be a wonderful year for all the media: a beautiful and charming young girl to photograph, an adoring older Prince, a fairy-tale wedding at St Paul's Cathedral and the announcement of a pregnancy. Given such a wealth of events, and the readiness of the happy couple to co-operate with the press, it is appalling that Lady Diana was nonetheless hounded with heartless insatiability. Prince Charles knew better than she did just what lay ahead of them both and even though she accepted his proposal early in 1981 he encouraged her to think it over during a month's visit to her mother in Australia. 'I wanted to give her time to consider

*One day old and already William is meeting the cameramen who will follow his movements with the persistence of hunters.*

whether it was all going to be too awful.' But she was only nineteen and deeply in love; an army of journalists and cameramen would not have frightened her off.

The engagement was announced on 24 February, to the great delight of millions all over the world. Very quickly, however, Diana showed she was not just a sweet and shy young thing. At her first public engagement at Goldsmiths Hall her revealing black gown testified to an independence of spirit which would not be easily quashed by royal conventions. And though Prince Charles has

always been the most biddable and conventional of the Queen's children he has been encouraged by his wife's fresh approach to break with tradition and dispense with formality when occasion demands it. His choice of St Paul's for the wedding, for example, was most unexpected and the kiss he gave his bride on the balcony of Buckingham Palace afterwards certainly had no precedent in the history of the House of Windsor. But although the Prince and Princess of Wales will go their own way in many small or personal things, they admire and honour the traditions of the royal family, which have been passed down from Queen Victoria and adapted by each generation. As Prince Philip was a breath of fresh air to the Queen's life, so is Diana to Prince Charles', but all her innovations will be against the backcloth of the united royal family. Margaret Trudeau, ex-wife of the Canadian prime minister, commented on the tough job which Diana has taken on: 'I do feel for her. What she has that I didn't have as a political wife is tremendous support from the family, from everyone.'

The new Princess of Wales needed that support when even after the dazzling wedding and the romantic honeymoon among the Greek islands, press interest still refused to simmer down. In early December 1981 the Queen held a conference of newspaper editors at Buckingham Palace to protest that the Princess could not even walk to the village shop without harrassment. 'Why can't the Princess send a servant to buy her wine gums?' asked the editor of *The News of the World*. 'That's the most pompous thing I have ever heard', said the Queen, to the delight of the other newspapermen. Unfortunately this frank exchange had little lasting effect. Only two months later, holidaying in the Bahamas, the Princess suffered her most distressing invasion of privacy so far when a photographer with a telephoto lens snapped her on the beach, in a bikini and very obviously pregnant. The papers concerned were forced to apologise but the Princess's

holiday had already been spoiled.

It was particularly unfortunate because the Princess was only just beginning to enjoy her pregnancy. The early months had been very unpleasant with severe morning sickness which took the healthy Diana by surprise. 'Why did no one tell me you felt like this?' she asked. After the announcement of her pregnancy on 5 November several of the Princess's engagements had to be cancelled or curtailed. Unexpectedly alone on his Cornish trip Prince Charles seemed unconcerned when reporters asked how Diana fared: 'You all have wives, you know the problems.' But though there was a respite in the middle of the month and they shared a visit to York where toys and baby clothes were heaped upon her, by the end of November she was under the weather again.

*Just before setting off for the other side of the world, Prince William's parents allowed photographers into their private apartments at Kensington Palace. Both pictures on these pages were taken on that occasion.*

It was not until mid-January that the Palace was able to announce: 'The Princess wants to carry out engagements for as long as she feels able and well enough.'

Although there was some surprise that the Prince and Princess of Wales had decided to begin their family immediately, the delight was universal. At a Guildhall luncheon on the day of the announcement the Lord Mayor likened their marriage to the everlasting lustre of 'a gold ingot that has now been supremely hallmarked by this morning's announcement that Your Royal Highnesses are to be blessed with a child, for which we all rejoice.' Lord Spencer spoke for the family: 'Diana wanted this child. She loves young people and they adore her. She will be a marvellous mother.'

The Princess was active up to the last moment of her pregnancy, glowing with health in pretty flowing dresses. On 21 June Prince Charles drove her through deserted streets at 5 am to the Lindo Wing of St Mary's, Paddington, where Princess Anne's children had been born. It was the quietest arrival the royal pair had ever known but the news was soon out and from 10 o'clock onwards flowers began

*Prince William arrives in Australia in the arms of Nanny Barnes, 1983. Four weeks later he gave the world's press a chance to photograph him in New Zealand (below, and opposite).*

to arrive in profusion. There were enormous bouquets from institutions and single roses from individual well-wishers. No mother can have had more warm and anxious thoughts turned towards her than Princess Diana in her first long labour.

No sooner had the nine o'clock news announced that there was no news, when the glad tidings came. A boy was

born, 'in marvellous form' according to his father and weighing just over 7lb. Members of the immediate royal family had to be tracked down all over the place to hear the news: the Queen was at Buckingham Palace but Prince Philip was in Cambridge, Princess Anne in the USA and Prince Andrew far south in the Falklands. Princess Margaret was at the Palace Theatre in London and received a rapturous ovation when the news was announced on stage.

Outside the hospital a cheering, singing crowd, drenched in champagne, awaited the departure of Prince Charles. Looking tired but happy the new father emerged at 11.30 pm, talked enthusiastically of his son and drove away for a well-earned rest at Kensington Palace. Later he described how it had affected him to be present at the birth: 'It is a rather grown up thing, I found. Rather a shock to my system.' Like all mothers the Princess had cared only that her child should be healthy and not at all what sex it was, but still it must have been a great satisfaction to produce the traditional heir within a year of her marriage. Despite the enormous popularity of nearly all England's queens there is still an illogical feeling that the burden of sovereignty falls more easily upon the shoulders of a man.

Less than twenty-four hours after the birth, mother and son left hospital and returned to Kensington Palace, part of which is the London home of the Prince and Princess of Wales. There is a courtyard there but no garden so like generations of nannies before her Miss Barbara Barnes has to take the little Prince into Kensington Gardens for some fresh air. Miss Barnes was thirty-nine at the time of her appointment and had been recommended by Lady Anne Tennant, lady-in-waiting to Princess Margaret. Lady Anne had found her calm, cheerful and charming, possessing 'a magical touch' with children. Miss Barnes was not at all overawed by her new responsibility: 'I treat all my children as individuals. I don't see any different problem in bringing up a royal baby.'

Her greatest difficulty will doubtless be how to share the care of Prince William with a devoted mother who would really like to be doing it all herself.

Prince William Arthur Philip Louis of Wales was christened as tradition demanded in the Music Room at Buckingham Palace wearing the Victorian lace robe made for Queen Victoria's eldest child in 1841. His godparents were King Constantine of Greece and Lord Romsey, distant cousins on Prince Philip's side of the family, Princess Alexandra, the Queen's first cousin, the Duchess of Westminster, Lady Susan Hussey and Laurens van der Post, an admired friend and mentor of Prince Charles. His first name was an unexpected choice but the parents had deliberately looked for a name the Prince could call his own, just as Charles had been the first Charles for many generations. 'We like the name William', the Prince of Wales explained, 'and it's a name that does not exist among close members of the family.' The baby's maternal grandparents were of course present at the christening, and Lord Spencer is determined that his share of the baby should not be overlooked. 'Prince

William will grow up close to the Spencer side of the family', he has said, 'and be influenced by them as much as by the Royals.' With this in mind he has already bought a seaside house in Sussex where younger members of the family can enjoy bucket and spade holidays.

No sooner was Prince William born than speculation began as to when his mother would present him with a brother or sister. A flying visit she made from Sandringham to a gynaecologist in the autumn of 1983 aroused hope of an announcement but it was not until February 1984 that her second pregnancy was confirmed. Once again the news was given early to the outside world, for the baby was not expected until late September.

Given the Princess's love of children, it is most unlikely that she will be content with only two babies. Prince Charles has said jokingly that her ambition was to produce more children than Queen Victoria but though she is young enough to do it, one suspects that common sense and financial pressures might call a halt at four.

But who can predict the future for a mother so determined not to be separated from her baby that before the age of nine months he had travelled further than most people travel in a lifetime? In March 1983 he flew to Australia with his parents and his nanny to be close at hand during their six-week tour. Previous generations of royal mothers had been wrenched away from their children for as much as six months but Diana proved that such separations are no longer necessary. Prince William did not accompany his parents on their travels in Australia itself but remained comfortably in their base at Woomargama. Although they saw little of him, the Australians were delighted to have William among them and gave him so many presents that most of them had to be distributed to Australian orphanages. Looking very brown and healthy, Prince William rejoined his parents for the flight to New Zealand and another two weeks of sunshine.

*Princess Diana carries her son at Aberdeen airport, October 1983.*

In the past royal parents have tried to protect their children as much as possible from the pressure of royal life until they are grown up. Perhaps the Princess of Wales will take the view that togetherness is more important than protective cocoons and an ever-increasing royal family will jet-set all over the world. Her own childhood was disturbed by the sad break-up of her parents' marriage so for her the unity of the family will be all-important. Prince Charles hopes in marriage to be as happy as his parents; for his children can he achieve an easier childhood than his own?

Whatever problems beset the royal couple as they struggle to bring up their children to be great and good, they will remember the strength of the family behind them, as the Queen expressed at her Silver Jubilee. 'A marriage begins by joining man and wife together. But this relationship, however deep, needs to develop and mature with passing years. For that it must be held firm in the web of family relationships, between parents and children, grandparents and grandchildren, cousins, aunts and uncles.' And for Charles and Diana there is an even greater family, millions of families in fact all over the world, who will share their hopes and their pleasures, sympathise with their setbacks, and surround them with love and affection all their days.

*A royal photocall, January 1984. William's ABC snow suit is a far cry from the trim little coats and bonnets in which his father was presented to the world. He set a new fashion, and stocks of a similar snow suit sold out within 24 hours of these pictures being published.*

# DESCENDANTS OF QUEEN VICTORIA

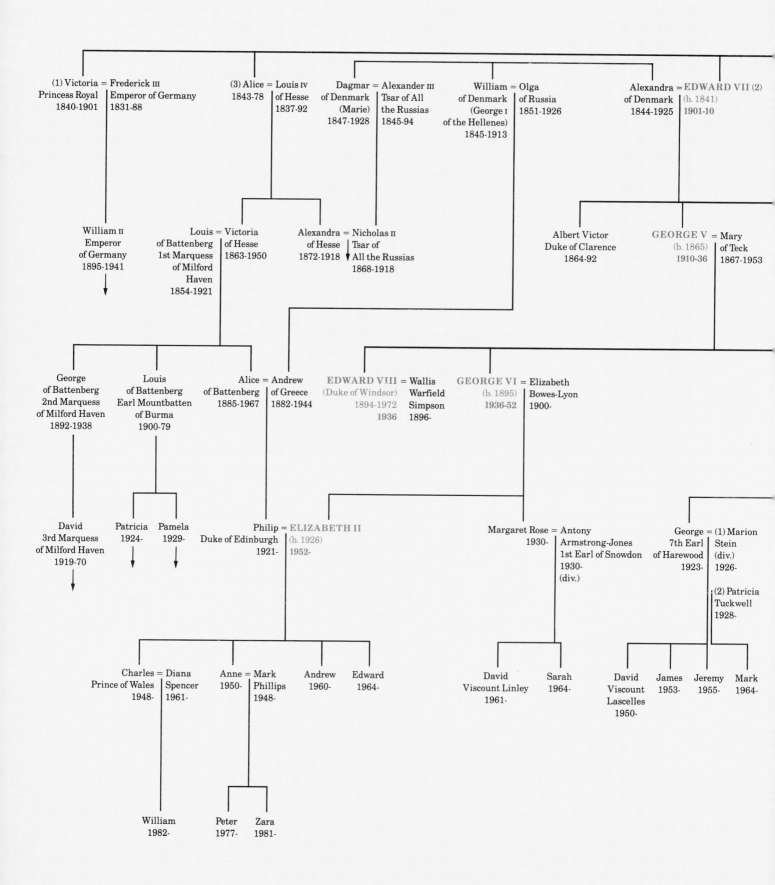

(1) Victoria = Frederick III
Princess Royal | Emperor of Germany
1840-1901 | 1831-88

(3) Alice = Louis IV
1843-78 | of Hesse
1837-92

Dagmar = Alexander III
of Denmark | Tsar of All
(Marie) | the Russias
1847-1928 | 1845-94

William = Olga
of Denmark | of Russia
(George I | 1851-1926
of the Hellenes)
1845-1913

Alexandra = EDWARD VII (2)
of Denmark | (b. 1841)
1844-1925 | 1901-10

William II
Emperor
of Germany
1895-1941

Louis = Victoria
of Battenberg | of Hesse
1st Marquess | 1863-1950
of Milford
Haven
1854-1921

Alexandra = Nicholas II
of Hesse | Tsar of
1872-1918 | All the Russias
1868-1918

Albert Victor
Duke of Clarence
1864-92

GEORGE V = Mary
(b. 1865) | of Teck
1910-36 | 1867-1953

George
of Battenberg
2nd Marquess
of Milford Haven
1892-1938

Louis
of Battenberg
Earl Mountbatten
of Burma
1900-79

Alice = Andrew
of Battenberg | of Greece
1885-1967 | 1882-1944

EDWARD VIII = Wallis
(Duke of Windsor) | Warfield
1894-1972 | Simpson
1936 | 1896-

GEORGE VI = Elizabeth
(b. 1895) | Bowes-Lyon
1936-52 | 1900-

David
3rd Marquess
of Milford Haven
1919-70

Patricia
1924-

Pamela
1929-

Philip = ELIZABETH II
Duke of Edinburgh | (b. 1926)
1921- | 1952-

Margaret Rose = Antony
1930- | Armstrong-Jones
| 1st Earl of Snowdon
| 1930-
| (div.)

George = (1) Marion
7th Earl | Stein
of Harewood | (div.)
1923- | 1926-
| (2) Patricia
| Tuckwell
| 1928-

Charles = Diana
Prince of Wales | Spencer
1948- | 1961-

Anne = Mark
1950- | Phillips
| 1948-

Andrew
1960-

Edward
1964-

David
Viscount Linley
1961-

Sarah
1964-

David
Viscount
Lascelles
1950-

James
1953-

Jeremy
1955-

Mark
1964-

William
1982-

Peter
1977-

Zara
1981-

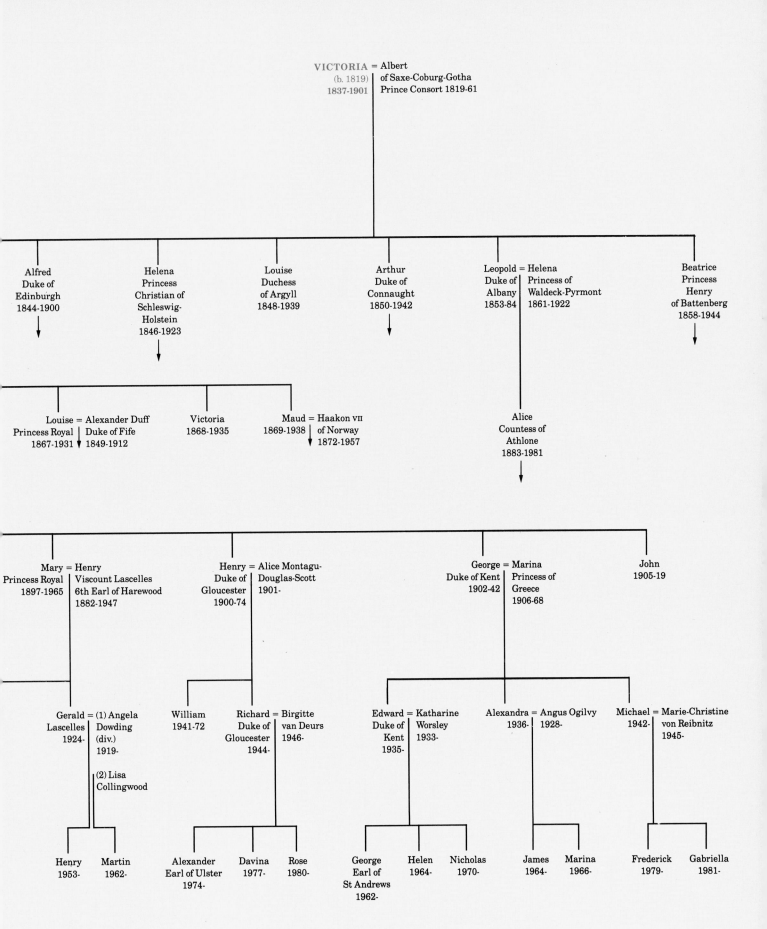

VICTORIA = Albert
(b. 1819) | of Saxe-Coburg-Gotha
1837-1901 | Prince Consort 1819-61

Alfred
Duke of
Edinburgh
1844-1900

Helena
Princess
Christian of
Schleswig-
Holstein
1846-1923

Louise
Duchess
of Argyll
1848-1939

Arthur
Duke of
Connaught
1850-1942

Leopold = Helena
Duke of | Princess of
Albany | Waldeck-Pyrmont
1853-84 | 1861-1922

Beatrice
Princess
Henry
of Battenberg
1858-1944

Louise = Alexander Duff
Princess Royal | Duke of Fife
1867-1931 | 1849-1912

Victoria
1868-1935

Maud = Haakon VII
1869-1938 | of Norway
1872-1957

Alice
Countess of
Athlone
1883-1981

Mary = Henry
Princess Royal | Viscount Lascelles
1897-1965 | 6th Earl of Harewood
1882-1947

Henry = Alice Montagu-
Duke of | Douglas-Scott
Gloucester | 1901-
1900-74

George = Marina
Duke of Kent | Princess of
1902-42 | Greece
1906-68

John
1905-19

Gerald = (1) Angela
Lascelles | Dowding
1924- | (div.)
| 1919-

(2) Lisa
Collingwood

William
1941-72

Richard = Birgitte
Duke of | van Deurs
Gloucester | 1946-
1944-

Edward = Katharine
Duke of | Worsley
Kent | 1933-
1935-

Alexandra = Angus Ogilvy
1936- | 1928-

Michael = Marie-Christine
1942- | von Reibnitz
| 1945-

Henry
1953-

Martin
1962-

Alexander
Earl of Ulster
1974-

Davina
1977-

Rose
1980-

George
Earl of
St Andrews
1962-

Helen
1964-

Nicholas
1970-

James
1964-

Marina
1966-

Frederick
1979-

Gabriella
1981-

Monarchs and their reigns printed in red

# ACKNOWLEDGEMENTS

Photographs and illustrations are supplied or reproduced by kind permission of the following (page numbers in italics indicate black-and-white illustrations):

Reproduced by gracious permission of Her Majesty the Queen 12, 14, 15, 17, 20 (left), 24, 27, 34, 38, 53 – from the Royal Collection; 4 (left), *16*, 18, 19, *22, 28* (bottom), 29 (top right), *30, 31, 32*, 33, 35, *36*, 43, *49* (top), *50* (bottom), *55, 57, 59*, 68 (centre right and bottom), 88 (bottom right) – from the Royal Archives, Windsor, copyright reserved;
BBC Hulton Picture Library *23* (top and bottom left), *25, 26, 40, 44, 45* (centre left), *46, 49* (bottom), *50* (top), *51* (top), *56, 60*, 61, *64, 65, 66, 67*, 68 (left), 69, 71, *74, 75, 77, 78, 79*, 81, *98, 100*;
BBC Copyright Photograph 87 (bottom);
British Museum 6, 8;
Camera Press 2 – Patrick Lichfield, 73 – Baron, 83 – Studio Lisa, 86 – Sir Cecil Beaton, 88 (bottom left) – John Vaughan, 89 (centre) – Patrick Lichfield, 92 – Patrick Lichfield, 102 – Norman Parkinson, 104 (bottom) – Snowdon, 105 – Snowdon, 106 (top) – Bryn Colton, 107 – Norman Parkinson, 108 – Sir Cecil Beaton, 109 – Roger Garwood, 110 (top) – Jim Bennett, 112 (bottom) – Snowdon, 113 – Patrick

Lichfield, 121 – Lionel Cherruault;
Reginald Davis 80, 82, 85, 87 (top), 91, 94 (top), 99, 103 (top), 104 (top);
The Department of the Environment 28 (top), 29 (centre and bottom);
Tim Graham 45 (top), 69 (bottom left), 95, 96, 97, 103 (bottom), 106 (bottom), 110 (bottom), 111, 112 (top), 114, 115, 116, 117, 118, 119, 120, 122, 123;
Guildhall Art Gallery 62–3;
Imperial War Museum 70;
Lambeth Palace Library 9;
Mansell Collection *23* (bottom right), *37, 39, 41, 45* (bottom), *47, 48, 51* (bottom);
National Gallery of Art, Washington; Andrew W. Mellon Collection 1937 (by Hans Holbein the Younger) 1;
National Portrait Gallery, London 13;
The Photo Source – Fox Photos *84, 101*; Colour Library International 5, 45 (centre right), 68 (top), 69 (bottom right), 88 (top), 89 (bottom), 93, 94 (bottom);
Popperfoto *76*, 90;
Press Association 89 (top);
Rijksmuseum, Amsterdam 7;
Topham 4 (right), 42, 52, 54, 58, 63 (top);
Victoria and Albert Museum, Crown Copyright 20–1;
The Trustees, the Wallace Collection, London 10–11

Picture Research by Sarah Waters

# INDEX